GW01091423

Microsoft®
Works Suite 99
At a Glance

Microsoft *Press*

Microsoft Works Suite 99 At a Glance

PUBLISHED BY
Microsoft Press
A Division of Microsoft Corporation
One Microsoft Way
Redmond, Washington 98052-6399

Library of Congress Cataloging-in-Publication Data
Busch, David D.
   Microsoft Works Suite At a Glance / Busch, David D.
       p.   cm.
   Includes index.
   ISBN 0-7356-0571-8
   1. Integrated software.   2. Microsoft Works. I. Title.
QA76.76.I57B87   1999
005.369—dc21
                                         98-31459
                                         CIP

Printed and bound in the United States of America.

1 2 3 4 5 6 7 8 9   QEQE   4 3 2 1 0 9

Distributed in Canada by ITP Nelson, a division of Thomson Canada Limited.

A CIP catalogue record for this book is available from the British Library.

Microsoft Press books are available through booksellers and distributors worldwide. For further information about international editions, contact your local Microsoft Corporation office, or contact Microsoft Press International directly at fax (425) 936-7329. Visit our Web site at mspress.microsoft.com.

Acquisitions Editors: Kim Fryer; Susanne Forderer
Project Editor: Jenny Moss Benson

Contents

Create a word processing
document.
See page 24

Change font and font size.
See page 46

*"How can I create
a table?"*

See page 58

*"How do I change
the size
of columns
or rows?"*

See page 76

Link or embed a spreadsheet in
another document.
See page 92

6 Tracking Information with Databases 95

7 Managing Events and Appointments with Works Calendar 115

Set appointment reminders.
See page 123

Set page margins.
See page 131

Saving favorite Web pages.
See page 150

"How do I fix a picture that is too dark?"

See page 196

"How can I find a good restaurant?"

See page 204

*"How do I
enter recurring
transactions?"*

See page 224

About This Book

Microsoft Works Suite 99 At a Glance is for anyone who wants to get the most from Microsoft Works 4.5, Microsoft Works Deluxe 99, and Microsoft Works Suite 99 with the least amount of time and effort. We think you'll find this book to be a straightforward, easy-to-read, and easy-to-use reference tool. With the premise that your computer should work for you, not you for it, this book's purpose is to help you get your work done quickly and efficiently so that you can take advantage of Microsoft Works while using your computer and its software to the max.

No Computerese!

Let's face it—when there's a task you don't know how to do but you need to get it done in a hurry, or when you're stuck in the middle of a task and can't figure out what to do next, there's nothing more frustrating than having to read page after page of technical background material. You want the information you need—nothing more, nothing less—and you want it now! And the information should be easy to find and understand.

That's what this book is all about. It's written in plain English—no technical jargon and no computerese. There's no single task in the book takes more than two pages. Just look up the task in the index or the table of contents, turn to the page, and there it is. Each task introduction gives you the information that is essential to performing the task, suggesting situations in which you can use the task or providing examples of the benefit you gain from completing the procedure. The task itself is laid out step by step and accompanied by a graphic that adds visual clarity. Just read the introduction, follow the steps, look at the illustrations, and get your work done with a minimum of hassle.

You may want to turn to another task if the one you're working on has a "See Also" in the left column. Because there's a lot of overlap among tasks, we didn't want to keep repeating ourselves; you might find elementary or more advanced tasks laid out on the pages referenced. We wanted to bring you through the tasks in such a way that they would make sense to you. We've also added some useful tips here and there and offered a "Try This" once in awhile to give you a context in which to use the task. But, by and large, we've tried to remain true to the heart and soul of the book, which is that the information you need should be available to you *at a glance*.

Useful Tasks...

Whether you use Works for work, play, or some of each, we've tried to pack this book with procedures for everything we could think of that you might want to do, from the simplest tasks to some of the more esoteric ones.

...And the Easiest Way to Do Them

Another thing we've tried to do in *Microsoft Works Suite 99 At a Glance* is to find and document the easiest way to accomplish a task. Works often provides many ways to accomplish a single result, which can be daunting or delightful, depending on the way you like to work. If you tend to stick with one favorite and familiar approach, we think the methods described in this book are the way to go. If you prefer to try out alternative techniques, go ahead! The intuitiveness of Works invites exploration, and you're likely to discover ways of doing things that you think are easier or that you like better. If you do, that's great! It's exactly what the creators of the Works Suite 99 software had in mind when they provided so many alternatives.

A Quick Overview

You don't have to read this book in any particular order. The book is designed so you can jump in, get the information you need, and then close the book, keeping it near your computer until the next time you need it. But that doesn't mean we scattered the information about with wild abandon. If you were to read the book from front to back, you'd find a logical progression from simple tasks to more complex ones. Those who own Microsoft Works Suite 99 will want to read the sections of this book dealing with the additional software included with the Suite version. You may find that some of the sections in this book don't apply to the version of Microsoft Works 99 that you own. To serve the broadest possible audience, *Microsoft Works Suite 99 At a Glance* covers all the applications available in the full suite. Perhaps those of you who purchased the other versions will find the descriptions herein so tempting that you'll upgrade! Here's a quick overview.

First, we assume that Microsoft Works is already installed on your machine. If it's not, the Setup program makes installation so simple that you won't need our help anyway. So, unlike most computer books, this one doesn't start out with installation instructions and a list of system requirements. You've already got that under control.

Section 2 of the book covers the basics: starting Microsoft Works; creating new documents; using wizards to automate document design; and performing simple functions like scrolling through documents, saving files, and using the easy Works Help system.

Sections 3 and 4 describe everything you need to know to begin creating documents with Works. Section 3 deals with the Works word processor, while Section 4 covers much of the same territory with Microsoft Word 97. Both sections describe entering and editing text; moving and copying text; formatting text for emphasis; creating and modifying tables; and checking your spelling.

Sections 5 and 6 describe creating and formatting spreadsheets and databases; entering information; copying, moving, or deleting data; calculating automatically and with formulas; and creating charts and reports.

Section 7 describes managing your appointments with Works Calendar; saving time by entering recurring appointments; setting reminders; and searching your calendar.

Section 8 describes printing with Works applications; formatting pages; setting margins, previewing pages; and selecting a printer.

Sections 9 and 10 describe working online with Microsoft Internet Explorer and Microsoft Outlook Express; connecting to the Internet; browsing the Web, creating a list of favorite sites; exchanging e-mail messages; and filing messages.

Section 11 describes preparing your own greeting cards with Graphics Studio Greetings 99; adding motion, music, and sound clips; and choosing artwork. You'll also learn how to use Picture It! Express to fine-tune pictures.

Section 12 describes the best ways to travel smarter with Expedia Streets 98; interpreting maps; finding addresses; and browsing restaurants and hotels.

Section 13 describes managing your finances with Money 99 Basic; setting up bank accounts; recording expenses; correcting errors; printing checks; reconciling accounts; and creating reports.

Section 14 describes researching with Encarta Encyclopedia 99; exploring cross-references; taking notes; saving results; browsing articles; and enjoying multimedia.

A Final Word (or Two)

I had three goals in writing this book. I want my book to help you:

◆ Do all the things you want to do with Works Suite 99.

◆ Discover how to do things you didn't know you wanted to do with Works Suite 99.

◆ Enjoy doing your work with Works Suite 99.

My "thank you" for buying this book is the achievement of those goals. I hope you'll have as much fun using *Microsoft Works Suite 99 At a Glance* as I've had writing it. The best way to learn is by doing, and that's what I hope you'll get from this book.

Jump right in!

2

Getting Started with Works 99

Getting started with Microsoft Works 99 is easy. The basic tools you'll use most to create documents, manage information, or communicate are clustered together under a single program, or *application*, where you can access them quickly. This integrated approach also makes it simple to switch back and forth among these main applications as you shift from word processing to spreadsheet to database to communications work. If you need some guidance, each Works tool is packed with pop-up tips, wizards to lead you through common tasks, and the most helpful Help window you've ever seen.

When you're ready to expand your horizons, Works 4.5, Works Deluxe 99, and Works Suite 99 include a rich selection of additional programs for use at work, at home, and at school. You can easily manage your finances with Microsoft Money 99 Basic; send and receive electronic mail with Microsoft Outlook Express; forage for information or entertainment on the World Wide Web with Microsoft Internet Explorer 4.0; do more sophisticated word processing with Microsoft Word 97; or organize your busy schedule with Microsoft Works Calendar. When holidays and vacations roll around, you can create your own greeting cards with Microsoft Graphics Studio Greetings 99, or plan a trip with Microsoft Expedia Streets 98.

Don't worry if you're not an expert in word processing, spreadsheets, or any of the other tools. If you know how to start your computer, navigate among folders and application icons, and have already installed Works, you're ready to begin.

Starting and Quitting Works

Works can be started and quit in the same way you start and quit other Microsoft Windows programs, by using the Start menu. If an icon for Works was placed on your desktop during installation, you can also start the program by double-clicking the icon.

SEE ALSO

For more information on how to save your work before exiting, see "Saving a File" on page 18.

TIP

Quit Works with a shortcut key or the Close button.
You can also quit Works by pressing Alt+F4, or by clicking the Close button (marked with an X) in the upper-right corner of the Works window.

Start Works 99

1. Click the Start button on the Windows taskbar.

2. Point to Programs.

3. Point to Microsoft Works.

4. Choose Microsoft Works.

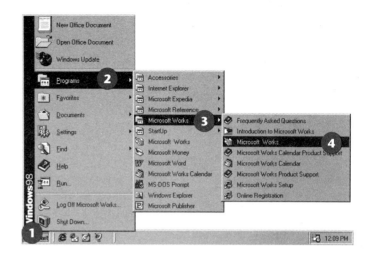

Quit Works 99

1. Choose Exit Works from the File menu.

Viewing the Works
Task Launcher Window

Click this tab to switch to another Works tool (Word Processor, Spreadsheet, Database, or Communications).

Click a category name to see or hide the wizards available for that category of document.

Click here to view wizards sorted in a different way: by category, in alphabetical order, by the most recently used, or by document type.

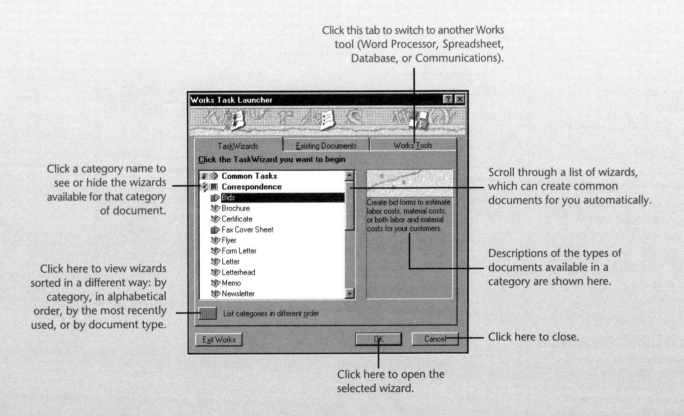

Scroll through a list of wizards, which can create common documents for you automatically.

Descriptions of the types of documents available in a category are shown here.

Click here to close.

Click here to open the selected wizard.

Opening an Existing Document

You'll frequently want to use a document you've worked on previously to add information or make other edits. You can open a document you've already created either with the Task Launcher or with the Open command on the File menu. Both methods open a dialog box that lets you navigate until you find the folder or file you're looking for. Works helps you quickly find and open your most recently used documents by listing them at the bottom of the File menu.

TRY THIS

Open recently used files.
Works displays the four most recently used files at the bottom of the File menu. You can quickly open any of them by clicking its name on the File menu.

Open an Existing Document from the File Menu

1. If the Task Launcher is visible, click the Cancel button to close it.

2. Choose Open from the File menu.

3. Navigate in the Open dialog box until you locate the folder and file you want to open.

4. Double-click the file you want to open.

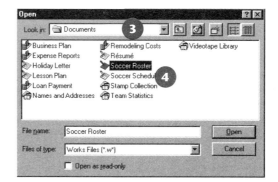

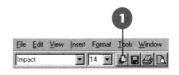

Launching tasks without a toolbar. *If there is no document open, the toolbar will not be visible. In that case, choose New from the File menu to open the Task Launcher.*

Open a document not listed under Existing Documents. *Click the Task Launcher button on the toolbar. Click the Existing Documents tab, and then click the Open A Document Not Listed Here button. Navigate in the Open dialog box until you locate the folder and file you want, and then double-click the name of the document you want to open.*

For information on locating a document, see "Find an Existing Document" on page 10.

Open an Existing Document with the Task Launcher

1. If the Task Launcher is not visible on your screen, click Task Launcher button on the toolbar.

2. Click the Existing Documents tab.

3. Double-click the name of the document you want to open.

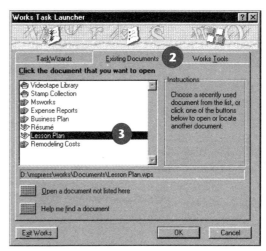

Finding an Existing Document

Often you'll want to find a document that is located in a folder on your hard disk. Works allows you to find existing documents based on the information you have about the file's location, filename, and text contents. You can search for a specific document or for groups of documents that share one or more properties.

TIP

Find recently edited documents. *To narrow your search to documents that have changed recently, click the Date tab, click the Find All Files button, and select Modified from the drop-down list box. Then choose a date range or the previous number of days or months to search.*

Find an Existing Document

1 If the Task Launcher is not visible on your screen, click the Task Launcher button on the toolbar.

2 Click the Existing Documents tab.

3 Click the Help Me Find A Document button.

4 Click the Name & Location tab if it isn't visible.

5 Type any text you want to search for within documents in the Containing Text text box.

6 To search a hard disk drive or folder other than your default hard disk drive, click a hard disk drive or folder in the Look In drop-down list box.

◆ Select the Include Subfolders check box to search within folders located inside the one you choose.

7 Click Find Now to begin your search.

8 Double-click the existing file you want to open.

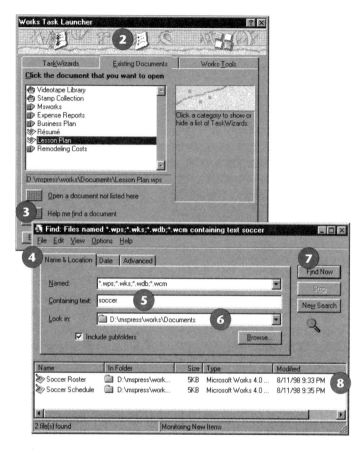

Creating a New Document from Scratch

There are three types of documents you can create with the Start From Scratch Wizard: word processing, spreadsheet, and database documents.

TIP

Choose documents created by a wizard. *After you select a wizard, you can choose from a list of documents you have already created with that wizard by clicking the Show Me A List Of Documents button in the Works Task Launcher dialog box.*

SEE ALSO

For more information on creating word processing documents, see "Opening Works Tools" on page 14.

Create a Document with the Start From Scratch Wizard

1. If the Works Task Launcher is not visible, click the Task Launcher button on the toolbar, or choose New from the File menu if the toolbar is not on the screen.

2. Click the TaskWizards tab if it is not visible.

3. Double-click the Start From Scratch Wizard in the Common Tasks category, and then click Yes, Run The TaskWizard.

4. Click either Word Processor, Spreadsheet, or Database to specify the kind of document you want to create. Click Next.

5. Use the drop-down lists to specify additional options for your documents.

6. Click the Create It! button to produce the document using the options you've chosen.

7. Review the check list of chosen options. Click Return To Wizard to change options or click the Create Document button to complete the document.

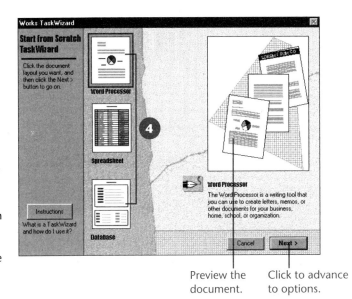

Preview the document.   Click to advance to options.

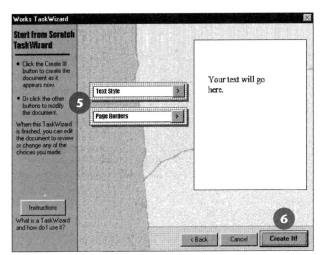

Creating a New Document with a TaskWizard

While Works allows you to create plain-vanilla documents without any help, TaskWizards can give you a head start to professional-looking documents. These helpers ask you a few questions and then automatically insert the elements you need to build a basic document in a variety of categories, such as Correspondence or Household. You can then edit the document by inserting, rearranging, or removing text, pictures, spreadsheet formulas, or other items. Works 99 includes wizards for the most common kinds of word processing documents, databases, and spreadsheets, so you can quickly create a report, manage names and addresses, or perform basic accounting tasks.

Choose a TaskWizard

1 Chose New from the File menu.

2 Click the TaskWizards tab if it is not visible.

3 Scroll through the list of wizards.

4 Double-click a wizard to run it.

Database wizards are indicated by a business card icon.

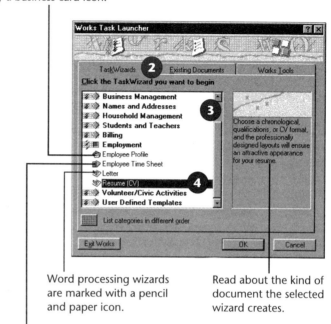

Word processing wizards are marked with a pencil and paper icon.

Spreadsheet wizards are marked with a calculator and pad icon.

Read about the kind of document the selected wizard creates.

Run a TaskWizard

1. Click the document layout you want.

2. Click the Next button in the lower-right corner of the wizard box.

   ◆ If you selected a wizard with no additional options, click the Create It! button instead to complete the document.

3. Click the Next button again.

4. Select the options and answer the questions to customize your document.

5. Click Create It! and view the check list showing the options you have selected.

   ◆ Click the Return To Wizard button to return to the options screen if you want to change any of the options.

6. Click the Create Document button to produce the document and return to the Works 99 main screen.

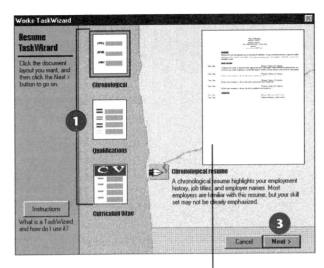

Preview the layout.

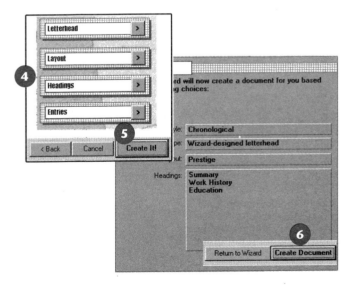

Opening Works Tools

A Microsoft Works tool helps you perform a task. Although TaskWizards automatically open the appropriate tool for a document you are creating, you may want to switch directly to a Works tool, usually to work on a different kind of document created with that tool. You can switch from one tool to another after you have already started using Works.

TIP

Switch to another open document. *To switch directly to a different open document regardless of which tool created it, click the Window menu and then click the name of the document from the list at the bottom of the menu.*

TIP

Switch to a new tool from the toolbar. *To create a new document using a different tool while working with any Works document, click the Task Launcher button on the toolbar.*

Open a Works Tool

1. If the Works Task Launcher is not visible, click the Task Launcher button on the toolbar, or choose New from the File menu if the toolbar is not visible.

2. Click the Works Tools tab.

3. Click the button marked with the tool you want to use.

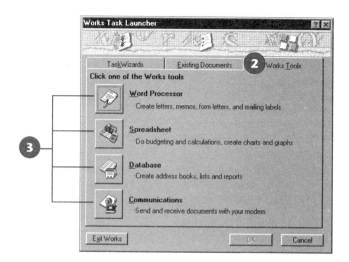

Navigating the Works Window

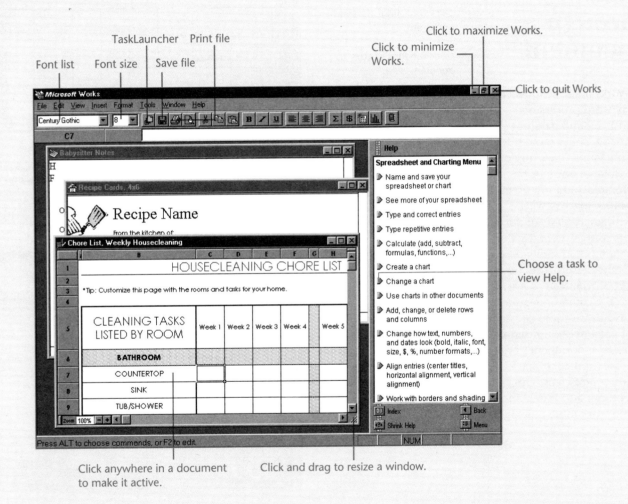

Font list

Font size

TaskLauncher

Save file

Print file

Click to minimize Works.

Click to maximize Works.

Click to quit Works

Choose a task to view Help.

Click anywhere in a document to make it active.

Click and drag to resize a window.

Microsoft Works

File Edit View Insert Format Tools Window Help

Century Gothic   8

C7

Babysitter Notes

Recipe Cards, 4x6

Recipe Name

From the kitchen of:

Chore List, Weekly Housecleaning

HOUSECLEANING CHORE LIST

*Tip: Customize this page with the rooms and tasks for your home.

CLEANING TASKS LISTED BY ROOM	Week 1	Week 2	Week 3	Week 4	Week 5
BATHROOM					
COUNTERTOP					
SINK					
TUB/SHOWER					

Zoom 100%

Press ALT to choose commands, or F2 to edit.

NUM

Help

Spreadsheet and Charting Menu

- Name and save your spreadsheet or chart
- See more of your spreadsheet
- Type and correct entries
- Type repetitive entries
- Calculate (add, subtract, formulas, functions,...)
- Create a chart
- Change a chart
- Use charts in other documents
- Add, change, or delete rows and columns
- Change how text, numbers, and dates look (bold, italic, font, size, $, %, number formats,...)
- Align entries (center titles, horizontal alignment, vertical alignment)
- Work with borders and shading

Index   Back

Shrink Help   Menu

Zooming and Scrolling Through a Document

The Works main window can display word processing, spreadsheet, and database documents at the same time, allowing you to view any or all of them at once, or to switch rapidly among them. The ability to work with three different kinds of documents using essentially the same menus and toolbars is one of the best features of Works 99. You need to learn how to use common features, such as how to zoom in and out of documents and scroll down longer documents, only once. This approach makes becoming proficient with Works easier and faster, and lets you work more quickly.

Zoom In and Out

1 Click the Zoom button to choose a magnification.

2 Click the Minus button to zoom out.

3 Click the Plus button to zoom in.

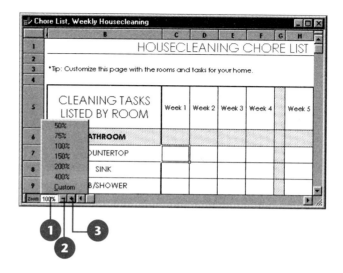

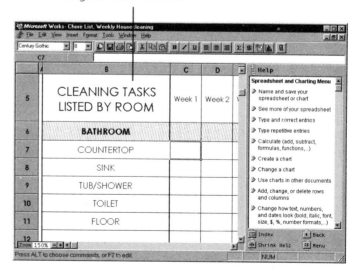

Image zoomed to 150%.

Split a document into two windows. *To split a document into two separately scrollable windows, drag the bar that appears just above the vertical scroll bar and just below the Close button. This allows you to view two parts of the document at once.*

Scroll through a Document

1. Use the scroll bars to move through the document.

Click and drag to move a document up or down quickly.

Click to scroll up by one screen.

Click to scroll up in your document by one line.

Click and drag the bar down to change the size of two separately scrollable windows.

Very short phone conversations:

Telemarketer: Hello. Have you considered putting aluminum siding on your home?
Me: Yeah, but now we're sort of used to the way the brick looks.
Telemarketer: Click.

Telemarketer: Is the little lady of the house in?
Me: No, she's in pre-school all morning.
Telemarketer: Click.

Telemarketer: May I speak to the person who's in charge of choosing a long distance service?
Me: No.
Telemarketer: Click.

Telemarketer: If you purchase a service contract on your new TV today, you can avoid hundreds of dollars in unforeseen repairs over the next 36 months.
Me: Mercy! I'm glad you told me this before the 30-day money-back period had expired!
Telemarketer: Click.

Telemarketer: Oh, if your wife isn't there, we'll call back at a time that's more convenient.
Me: More convenient for you or for her?

Click to scroll down by one screen.

Click to scroll down in your document by one line.

Click the same elements in the horizontal scroll bar to scroll horizontally.

2

Saving a File

Saving your document frequently is your first line of defense against losing your work because of mishaps, such as a computer failure or power outage, or even human error. The hard disk that stores your document can malfunction, a power brownout lasting only a second can cause your computer to restart, or you can simply neglect to save your document when you quit Works, even though the program always reminds you to do so. You can quickly save the current version of the active document, or save it under a new name to preserve a document at a particular stage of your work, in case you want to go back to the earlier version at any time.

Save a File

1. Make the document you want to save active by clicking anywhere within the document's window.

2. To save a new file, or to save a file under a new name, choose Save As from the File menu.

   ◆ If the document has already been saved, click the Save button on the toolbar.

3. Type a new name in the File Name text box or select a new folder in which to save the file.

4. Click the Save button.

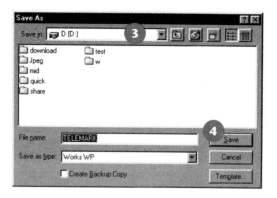

Getting Help

Works offers several ways to get help with what you're doing. You can summon a pop-up window of information dealing with your current task at the press of a key. Works offers a menu of helpful hints that you can keep on display for instant reference.

TIP

Access Help for the current task. *Press F1 to receive help related to whatever task you're currently performing.*

TIP

Move through Help Index quickly. *When viewing the Help Index, type the first letter of the topic you want to view to skip to that section in the Help list; type more of the topic name to jump directly to that topic and related topics.*

Get Help from the Help Menu

1. Scroll through the Help menu to locate the general topic you need help with.

2. Click the arrow next to the general topic to reveal a more detailed list of related topics.

   ◆ Click the Back button to return to the previous Help screen.

   ◆ When viewing topics, the Step-by-Step and More Info tabs provide additional aid.

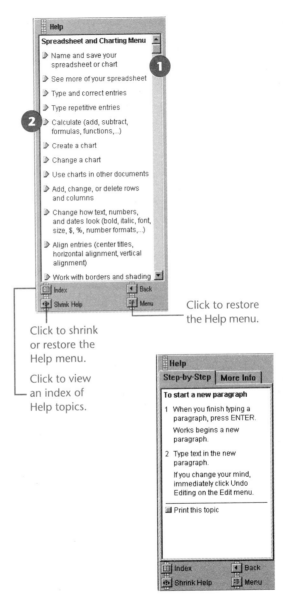

Click to restore the Help menu.

Click to shrink or restore the Help menu.

Click to view an index of Help topics.

Searching for Help Topics

You can also search through a comprehensive Help file by using keywords. You can type a word or two to view topics pertaining to that word or phrase.

Search for Help in the Help Index

1 Click the Index button on the Help menu to open the Index dialog box.

2 Click the Index tab if it is not visible, and then type a word for the action you want to learn about to review a list of all topics relating to that word.

3 Click the Contents tab to view a list of folders containing topics arranged by the type of task.

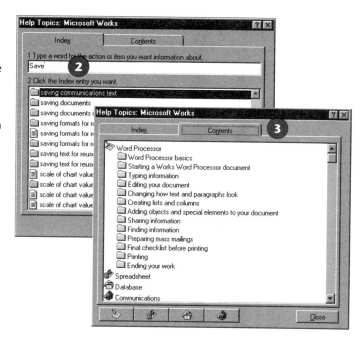

3

Word Processing with Works

It's hard to imagine a world without word processing, but only 15 to 20 years ago, most letters, memos, forms, and other personal or business documents were created with typewriters. Today, word processing is one of the top uses for personal computers. You can create a perfect letter with no spelling errors, strike-throughs, or unsightly patches of erasing fluid. You can put graphics or charts on a page, choose type styles, and arrange text with multiple columns to create a newsletter. Editing your work—even if you make extensive changes—is a point-and-click or drag-and-drop operation. The "processing" part of word processing includes time-saving automated features that can set line spacing, place line and page breaks in the right places, as well as find words or phrases and replace them with other text. You can dress up pages by applying one of Works' built-in formats or one you design with font, margins, alignment, or other attributes. The Works word processor makes it easy to perform the most common tasks.

Viewing the
Word Processor

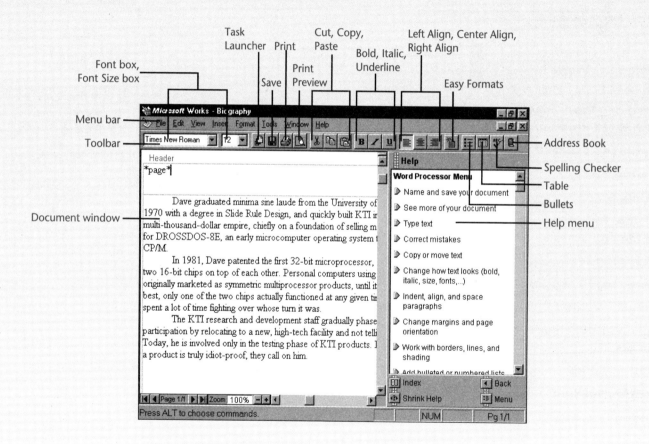

Font box,
Font Size box

Task
Launcher Print

Save

Print
Preview

Cut, Copy,
Paste

Bold, Italic,
Underline

Left Align, Center Align,
Right Align

Easy Formats

Menu bar

Toolbar

Document window

Address Book

Spelling Checker

Table

Bullets

Help menu

Comparing Works and Other Word Processors

The Microsoft Works word processor tool shares many of the same functions with Microsoft Word and other word processors. All allow entering text, editing and moving text, formatting with fonts in different sizes and styles, and previewing documents as they will look when printed. However, Works differs from Word and other word processors in several important respects. These include:

- ◆ Works tools are integrated. You can have word processing, spreadsheet, or database documents all open on your screen at one time, switch between them, and work with them using toolbars and menus that are similar.

- ◆ Works is easier to learn. It takes only a few minutes to learn how to use most features you need.

- ◆ Works is easier to use. The most important features can be activated by clicking a button on the toolbar. Others can be selected from simple menus on the menu bar.

- ◆ Help is always available. Works' Help menu can remain on-screen at all times, ready for immediate reference if you need guidance to complete a task.

- ◆ The streamlined set of features is easier to master. Works has fewer features than Microsoft Word 97, yet still contains the capabilities required to perform the majority of common tasks. That makes Works easier to learn, so you can quickly become a Works pro. Works includes Microsoft Word 97 for those who need more advanced capabilities, such as enhanced mail-merging facilities or fancier layouts for newsletters or other projects.

3

Creating a Document

All new Works documents are created in much the same way, so once you learn how to create a word processing document, you'll know how to create a spreadsheet or database by using the other Works tools. You can create a blank word processing document no matter which Works tool you are using. If you're working on a spreadsheet, you can switch to a new word processing document, or vice versa. A new, blank document is given a generic name, such as Unsaved Document 1, which you can change to any name you like by saving the document to your hard disk drive.

TIP

Start a new document with the Task Launcher button. *If the Works toolbar is visible, click the Task Launcher button, click the Works Tools tab, and then click the Word Processor button.*

Create a New Document

1. Choose New from the File menu.

2. Click the Works Tools tab.

3. Click the Word Processor button.

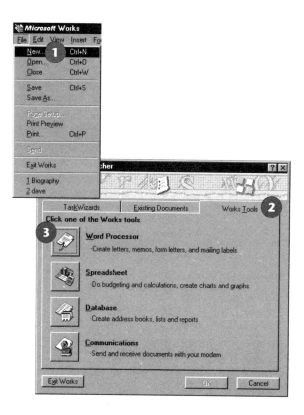

Entering Text

Typing text is the first step to creating a document in the Works word processor. You place the cursor where you want to begin typing, and enter text. Pressing the Backspace key moves the cursor to the left, and removes characters at the same time. Works automatically wraps text around to the next line when you reach the right margin.

TIP

Set a starting point for typing. *When the insertion point is within the document area, it changes into a large I shape. Clicking in the document sets the mouse pointer, or cursor, which is a large vertical bar that marks the place where you can start typing.*

SEE ALSO

See "Formatting Paragraphs" on page 30 for information on how to specify space between paragraphs as you type.

Enter Text

1. Click to place the insettion point in the document, below the area marked Header.

2. Type the text you want to enter. Do not press the Enter key at the end of each line.

3. Press Enter at the end of each paragraph to begin a new paragraph on the next line. Press Tab at the beginning of the new paragraph to produce an indent.

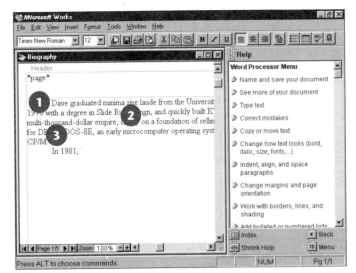

Editing Text

To modify text you have already typed, you must first select the characters, words, phrases, sentences, or paragraphs you want to replace. Selected text is shown in a document by highlighting. Highlighting reverses the colors used to display the text from black characters on a white background to white characters on a black background. Works has easy methods for quickly selecting characters, words, phrases, whole sentences, entire paragraphs, or the complete document. Once you have selected text, you can replace it by typing.

TIP

Add text to a selection. *To add more text to a high-lighted selection, hold down the Shift key while dragging the insertion point through the additional text to be selected.*

Replace the Text

1 Select the text to be changed.

2 Replace the selected text by typing.

SELECTING TEXT	
To highlight	**Do this**
An entire word	Double-click anywhere in the word.
A phrase	Drag the insertion point through the phrase.
A sentence	Hold down the Ctrl key and click anywhere in the sentence.
A full line	Click in the margin to the left of the line.
A paragraph	Double-click in the margin to the left of the line.
An entire document	Choose Select All from the Edit menu.

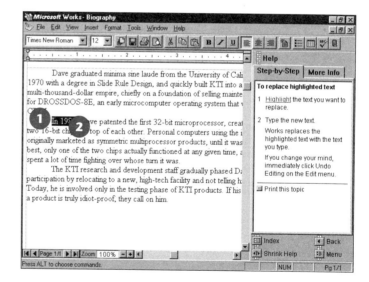

Copying, Cutting, and Moving Text

When you copy text, the text remains in its original location, and a duplicate is placed on the Windows Clipboard. You can paste the copy of the text in one or multiple new locations. When you cut text, the text is removed from its current location and placed on the Windows Clipboard, and can be pasted to move the text.

TIP

Remove text completely.
To remove text completely from a document, select the text to be deleted, and click the Cut button.

TIP

Paste multiple copies.
Once text has been copied to the Clipboard, it remains there until it is replaced with new text. You can paste text from the Clipboard in multiple locations.

Copy or Move Text

1. Select the text to be copied or moved.

2. Click the Copy button on the toolbar to copy the text, or the Cut button to move the text.

3. Click at the location where you want to insert the text.

4. Click the Paste button on the toolbar.

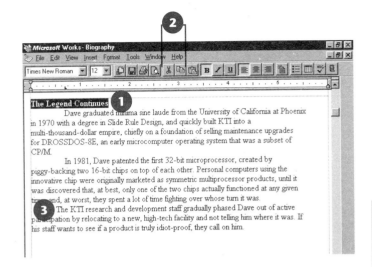

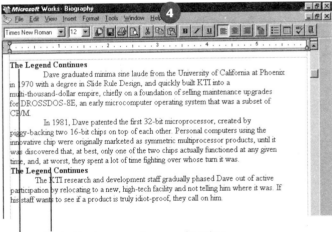

Pasted text appears in a new location.

Original text is copied in its original location.

3

Formatting Text

You can format individual characters, words, phrases, paragraphs, or even an entire document using the text font, size, and style features in Works. Select the text you want to change, and then choose the kind of formatting you want from the toolbar. Additional styles are available on the Format menu.

TIP

Find a font quickly. *To find a font quickly, click the Font drop-down arrow, and then type the first few characters of the font's name. The list will move to the first font matching those characters, and you can then select the font by clicking its name.*

TIP

Remove font formatting. *To remove bold, italic, or underline formatting from text, select the text and then click the Bold, Italic, or Underline buttons on the toolbar.*

Choose a Text Font

1. Select the text you want to format.

2. Click the Font drop-down arrow and choose a font from the list.

Choose a Standard Text Size and Formatting

1. Select the text you want to format.

2. Click the Font Size drop-down arrow and choose a size from the list.

3. If the text size you want is not shown, type the size you want in the Font Size box, and then press Enter.

4. Click the Bold, Italic, or Underline toolbar button to apply that style.

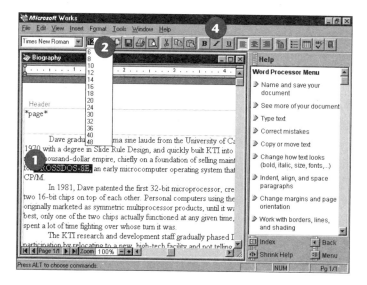

TIP

Preview fonts on the toolbar. *Choose Options from the Tools menu, click the View tab, and then click the Preview Fonts In Toolbar button to show the fonts as they will actually look in the Font drop-down list.*

Specify Other Styles or a Font Color

1 Select the text you want to format.

2 Choose Font And Style from the Format menu.

3 Select the Strikethrough check box to specify crossed-out text.

4 Click the Superscript or Subscript option button to create superscript or subscript text.

5 Click the Color drop-down arrow and choose a color from the list to specify a color for the selected text.

6 Click OK to apply the formatting.

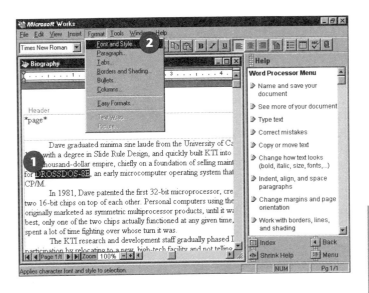

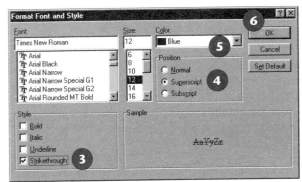

Formatting Paragraphs

To help your documents look the way you intend, you'll want to specify how much space appears between each line, how the text is indented and aligned, and the position of the tab stops that line up indents and columns. Line spacing allows you to pack more information on a page with single spacing, or spread out the lines with double spacing or another value. Indentations and tabs can make paragraphs stand out from each other, and you can arrange information for material like tables in neat columns. To format paragraphs, you need to select the paragraphs to be formatted, and then apply one of the paragraph formatting options.

Adjust Line Spacing

1. Select the paragraphs to be spaced.

2. Choose Paragraphs from the Format menu.

3. Click the Spacing tab, if necessary.

4. In the Line Spacing box, click the up or down arrow to select the spacing you want.

5. Click OK to apply the spacing.

Click to keep Works from inserting a page break between this paragraph and the one that follows.

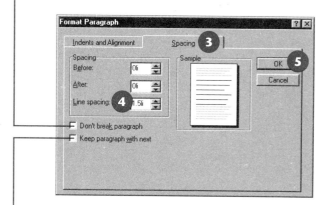

Click to keep Works from inserting a page break within a paragraph.

Align Text

1. Select the paragraphs you'd like to align.

2. Click the Left Align, Center Align, or Right Align buttons on the toolbar to align the text flush left/ragged right, centered, or flush right/ragged left, respectively.

Left Align.

Center Align.

Right Align.

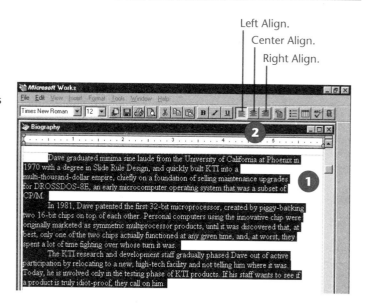

TIP

Use Ruler for the first time. *The first time you use the Ruler, the First-Time Help box appears with information about using the Ruler.*

TIP

Set decimal line spacing. *Lines do not have to be spaced in whole numbers. You can type decimal numbers, such as 1.5, 1.66, 2.5, and so forth, to fine-tune the spacing between your lines.*

TIP

Add, move, or delete tabs. *Select the paragraph(s) where you want to add or modify tab stops. Add a left-aligned tab by clicking the Ruler at the position you'd like to place the tab. To add a decimal, center-aligned, or right-aligned tab, double-click the ruler at its position and choose alignment from the Format Tabs dialog box. Drag the icon left or right to move a tab; drag the icon off the ruler to delete it.*

SEE ALSO

See "Creating Tables" on page 36 for information on using Works' table features.

Adjust Indentation

1. Select the paragraph you want to indent.

2. Choose Paragraph from the Format menu.

3. Click the Indents And Alignment tab.

4. Click the up or down arrow to select the amount of indentation.

   ◆ In the Left box, type the amount of indentation applied on the left side of all the lines in the paragraph.

   ◆ In the Right box, type the amount of indentation applied on the right side of all the lines in the paragraph.

   ◆ In the First Line box, type the amount of indentation applied only to the first line of the paragraph.

5. Choose Alignment (either Left, Center, Right, or Justified).

6. Click OK.

Click the Left, Center, Right, or Justified option button to align the paragraph.

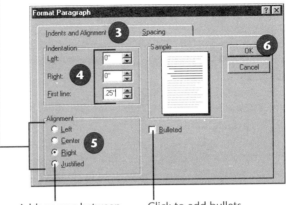

Adds spaces between words on each line to align the text at both the right and left margins.

Click to add bullets to the paragraph.

Formatting Pages

Formatting a page allows you to apply a consistent style to the margins, headers (which appear at the top of the page), footers (which appear at the bottom of the page), and other elements. Works includes a Page Setup dialog box that allows you to quickly set margins. You can type headers and footers in the spaces provided for them at the top and bottom of each page. You can also automatically insert page numbers as well as the date or time on each page in the location you specify.

Set Margins

1. Choose Page Setup from the File menu.

2. Click the Margins tab.

3. Specify measurements for the top, bottom, right, and left margins.

4. Click OK to apply the margins.

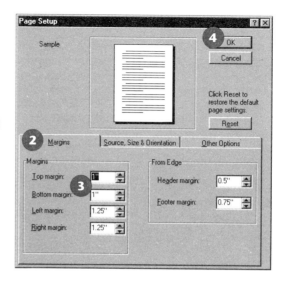

Align header or footer.
*Headers or footers can be
aligned at the left or right
margins, or centered, by
selecting the header or footer
and clicking the Left Align,
Right Align, or Center Align
button on the toolbar.*

**Use multiple-line headers
or footers.** *Headers or footers
can consist of more than one
line of text. Works expands the
area at the top or bottom of
the page where they are displayed if they are longer than
one line. A header or footer can
occupy as much as one-third of
each page.*

**Insert the document
name in the header or
footer.** *Often, it's useful to
include the name of the document in the header or footer.
To add this information, place
the insertion point in the header
or footer, and choose Document
Name from the Insert menu.
Works inserts the text *filename*
and replaces it with the actual
name of the document each
time it is printed.*

Add a Header and Footer

1. Move the insertion point
to the top of the page (for
a header) or to the bottom
of the page (for a footer).

2. In the header or footer
area, type the text you
want to appear.

3. To insert an automatically
updated page number,
choose Page Number from
the Insert menu.

4. To insert an automatically
updated date or time,
choose Date And Time
from the Insert menu.

   ◆ Select a date or time
   format.

   ◆ Click the Automatically
   Update When Printed
   check box to have
   Works use the current
   date or time when the
   document is printed.

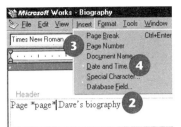

Applying Ready-Made Formats

Works includes ready-made formats for font, font size, typeface, borders, shadings, paragraph indentations or margins, and tabs you can apply to paragraphs in a document. Works includes more than two dozen formats for headings, mastheads, flyer text, and other common paragraph attributes. You can also easily create your own formats to reuse within the same document or other documents.

Apply a Format

1 Select the text you want to format.

2 Click the Easy Format button on the toolbar.

3 When the Easy Format menu appears, if the format you want is shown in the list of the five most recently used formats, select it to apply that format. Otherwise click More Easy Formats.

4 Scroll down the list of formats.

5 Click the format you want.

6 Click the Apply button to format the text you selected.

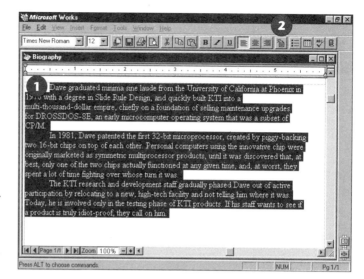

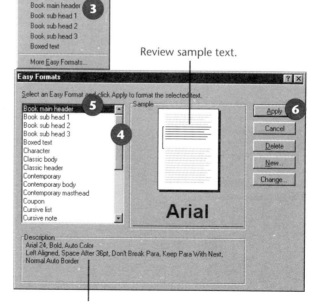

Review sample text.

Attributes of the selected format

TIP

Create a format from a selection. *You can turn any paragraph's current attributes into a format by selecting the paragraph, clicking the Easy Format button, and then choosing Create From Selection from the Easy Format menu.*

SEE ALSO

See "Formatting Text" on page 28, and "Formatting Paragraphs" on page 30 for more information on setting font and paragraph attributes.

Create a New Format

1. Click the Easy Format button on the toolbar.

2. Choose More Easy formats

3. Click the New button.

4. Enter a name for the new format.

5. Click the Font button and choose a typestyle.

6. Click the Borders button and select a border type.

7. Click the Shading button.

8. Click the Paragraph button and choose indents and alignment.

9. Click the Bullets button and choose a style of bullet, bullet size, and indentation.

10. Click the Tabs button and specify any tabs you want for the paragraph.

11. Click Done when you are finished defining the new format to return to the Easy Format dialog box.

12. Click the Apply button in the Easy Format dialog box to return to your document.

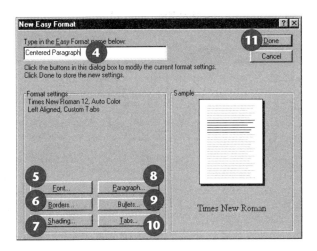

Creating Tables

Tables are an easy way to arrange information in your document in rows and columns. Works tables can be used to sort text and numbers or to perform calculations on rows and columns, just as you can with a spreadsheet. A table is a good formatting choice when your document will consist of mostly text, but will include information, such as a list of names and phone numbers, which can be set up in tabular form. Before creating a table, you should first look at your information to see how many rows and columns you'll need. You can always add new rows or columns later, but planning a basic format first can save time.

Create a Table

1 Click in the document where you want to insert the table.

2 Click the Insert Table button.

3 Click the up or down arrow to select the number of rows.

4 Click the up or down arrow to select the number of columns.

5 Scroll through the Select A Format list and choose a format for your table.

6 Click OK to create the table.

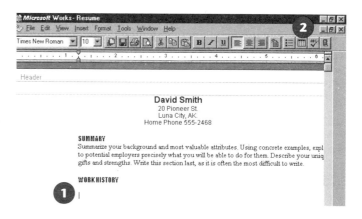

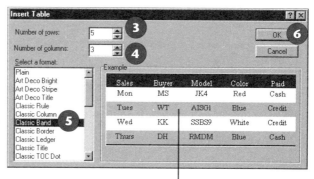

Preview of table appears here.

Enter Text or Numbers into a Table

1 Click anywhere in the table to select it.

2 Click in any cell to enter information into it, or to change information already in it.

Add Columns or Rows

1 Click in the table to select it.

2 Click in the gray column heading to the right of where you want to add a column, or click in the gray row heading below where you want to add a row.

3 Choose Insert Column or Insert Row from the Insert menu.

Checking Spelling

Works can improve the accuracy of your documents by searching for misspelled words, incorrect capitalization or hyphenation, and some frequent errors in composition, such as repeated words. Although Works knows the correct spelling for thousands of words, you can add words, such as specialized or technical terminology relating to your job, to a personal dictionary. As you use Works, your personal dictionary will become larger and richer if you take the time to add words to it.

Check Your Spelling

1. Click where you'd like Works to begin checking your spelling in a document. If you want to check the entire document, click at the beginning.

2. Click the Spelling Checker button on the toolbar.

3. Click the correct spelling on the scrolling Suggestions list, or type the correct spelling in the Change To box.

4. Click Change to change the misspelled word to the correct spelling.

5. Click Change All to change all occurrences of the misspelled word in the current document.

6. Click Ignore to ignore the word without changing its spelling.

7. Click Ignore All to ignore every instance of the word in your document.

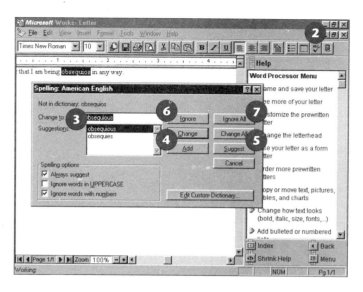

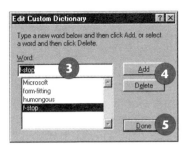

TIP

Add words while checking spelling. *To add words while performing a spelling check, click Add when the word appears in the Spelling dialog box.*

TIP

Change spelling dictionaries. *To change to a different dictionary, perhaps a specialized dictionary supplied with another program, choose Options from the Tools menu, click the Proofing Tools tab, and then choose the dictionary you want from the Choose Dictionary drop-down list.*

TIP

Find a better word. *Works can also help you locate an alternate word for one you are using. Select the word, and then choose Thesaurus from the Tools menu. A list of words with a similar meaning appears. If you want to use the synonym in the Replace With Synonym box, click the Replace button.*

TIP

Ignore all occurrences. *Click the Ignore All button when your document uses a word that is not in Works' dictionary, but is correctly spelled.*

Add or Delete Words from Your Personal Dictionary

1 Choose Spelling from the Tools menu.

2 Click Edit Custom Dictionary.

3 Type the word you want to add or delete in the Word box.

4 Click Add or Delete to add the word to or remove the word from your personal dictionary.

5 Click Done when finished.

6 Click Cancel to close the Spelling dialog box.

Printing Documents

Works uses the same procedures to print documents with all its tools, so once you've learned the method for one tool, you can apply the same method to the others. You can select a printer (if you have more than one printer connected to your computer, or your computer is on a network), preview a document too see how it will look when printed, select pages or page ranges to print, and choose from other options. If you print several copies of a document, Works can collate the pages by printing them in order multiple times.

TIP

Preview a document. *To see how a document will look before it is printed, click the Print Preview button on the toolbar.*

Print a Document

1. Choose Print from the File menu.

2. In the Print Range area, click the All option button to print all of the pages in the document, or click the Pages button and enter the page range you want to print.

3. In the Copies area, type the number of copies you would like to print.

4. Click the Collate check box if you are printing more than one copy of a document, and want the pages collated.

5. Click OK to print.

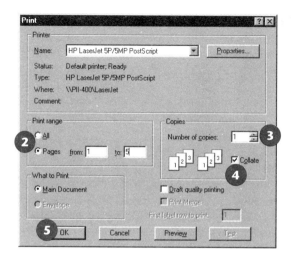

4

Word Processing with Word 97

Microsoft Word 97 is the full-featured word processing program included with Microsoft Works Suite 99. Word has more advanced features than the Works word processor, including more options for tables, as well as sophisticated layout features for creating multicolumn newsletters and other publications. Word 97 includes more than a dozen toolbars, and can be easily customized to include the toolbar buttons for the features you use the most. The program relies less on wizards for starting new documents, and the large on-screen Help menu is replaced by a compact Office Assistant that provides information and how-to-do-it instructions. Like the Works word processor, Word 97 is easy to learn and use, and is an excellent option if you are looking for additional features to improve the appearance of your word processing documents.

Creating a Document

When you create a new document, Word opens a blank page. Like the Works word processor, as you type and fill the blank page, Word creates new pages for you to hold all your text. Word assigns a generic name to new documents, such as Document1, which remains until you save the document with a new name.

TIP

Use Page Layout view.
Word displays new documents as one continuous page, with dotted lines indicating a page break. If you'd rather see the pages as they will appear when printed, choose Page Layout from the View menu. Choose Normal from the View menu to return to the continuous page view. Word remembers the view you used last, and restores it when you next open the document.

Create a New Document

1 Click the New button on the toolbar.

Entering Text

To enter text into a Word document, you place the insertion point on your screen at the position where you want to begin typing. As you type, you can use the Backspace key to delete characters while moving the cursor to the left. Word wraps text around to the next line when you reach the right margin, and inserts a new page when you reach the bottom of the current page.

TIP

Set a new starting point for typing. *Word places the insertion point at the beginning of a new document, so you can begin typing immediately (the insertion point can't go anywhere else on an empty page). If you want to enter text in another location on a page that already has some text on it, click in the location where you'd like to set the insertion point.*

Enter Text

1. Click to place the insertion point in the document.

2. Type the text you want to enter. Do not press the Enter key at the end of each line.

3. Press the Enter key at the end of each paragraph to begin a new paragraph on the next line. Press the Tab key at the beginning of the new paragraph to indent it.

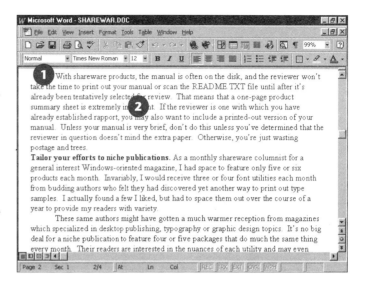

4

Editing Text

To modify text you have already typed, you must first select the characters, words, phrases, sentences, or paragraphs you want to replace. Selected text is shown in a word document by highlighting. Highlighting reverses the colors used to display the text from black characters on a white background to white characters on a black background. Word uses the same methods as Works for quickly selecting characters, words, phrases, whole sentences, entire paragraphs, or the complete document. Once you have selected text, you can replace it by typing.

TIP

Add text to a selection. *To add more text to a highlighted selection, hold down the Shift key while dragging the insertion point through the additional text to be selected.*

Select Characters, a Word, a Phrase, or a Paragraph

SELECT TEXT	
To highlight	**Do this**
An entire word	Double-click anywhere in the word.
A phrase	Drag the insertion point through the phrase with the mouse.
A sentence	Hold down the Ctrl key and click anywhere in the sentence.
A full line	Click in the margin to the left of the line.
A paragraph	Double-click in the margin to the left of the line.
An entire document	Choose Select All from the Edit menu.

Replace Selected Text

1. Select the text to be replaced.

2. Replace the selected text by typing.

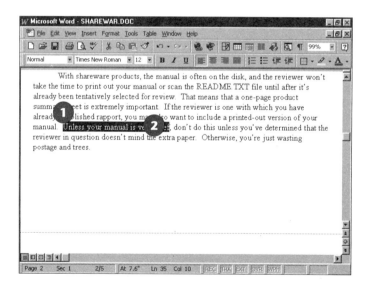

Copying, Cutting, and Moving Text

Word operates in the same way as Works and other Windows applications when copying text. The text you copy remains in its original location in the document, and a duplicate is placed on the Windows Clipboard. You can then paste the copy of the text in one or multiple new locations. When you cut text, the text is removed from its current location and placed on the Windows clipboard. You cut text when you want to remove it completely from the document, or move it to another location by pasting it. When you paste text, any text on the Clipboard that you have copied or cut is put in the current position of the insertion point. Text remains on the Clipboard until it is replaced with new text, so you can paste the same text multiple times.

Copy or Move Text

1. Select the text to be copied or moved.

2. Click the Copy button on the toolbar to copy the text, or the Cut button to move the text.

3. Click at the location where you want to insert the text.

4. Click the Paste button on the toolbar.

Original text stays where it was.

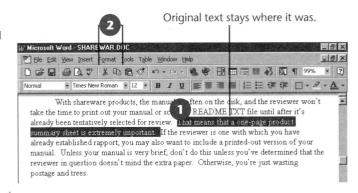

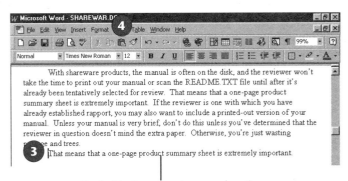

Copied text appears in a new location.

Formatting Text

You can format individual characters, words, phrases, paragraphs, or even an entire document using the text font, size, and style features in Word. You select the text you want to change, and then choose the kind of formatting you want from the toolbar. Additional styles are available on the Format menu.

Choose a Text Font

1. Select the text you want to format.

2. Click the Font drop-down arrow and choose a font from the list.

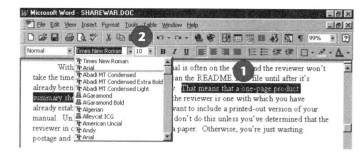

Choose a Standard Text Size and Formatting

1. Select the text you want to format.

2. Click the Font drop-down arrow and choose a font.

3. Click the Font Size drop-down arrow and choose a size from the list.

   ◆ If the text size you want is not shown, type the size you want in the Font Size box, and then press Enter.

4. Click the Bold, Italic, or Underline toolbar button to apply that style.

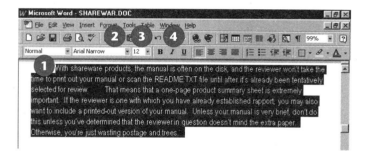

Apply underlining. *You can choose several styles of underlining, including single, double, thick, or dotted, from the Underline drop-down list on the Fonts tab of the Font dialog box.*

Find a font quickly. *To find a font quickly, click the Font drop-down arrow, and then type the first few letters of the font's name. The list will move to the first font matching those letters, and you can then select the font by clicking its name.*

Add or remove font formatting. *To add or remove bold, italic, or underline formatting from text, select the text and then click the Bold, Italic, or Underline button on the toolbar.*

Specify Other Styles or a Font Color

1. Select the text you want to format.

2. Choose Font from the Format menu. Click the Font tab if it is not visible.

3. Click the Strikethrough or Double Strikethrough check box to specify single or double crossed-out text.

4. Click the Superscript or Subscript check box to create superscript or subscript text.

5. Click the Color drop-down arrow and choose a color from the list to specify a color for the selected text.

6. Click the Shadow, Outline, Emboss, or Engrave check box to choose those attributes.

7. Click the Small Caps or All Caps check box to capitalize the text.

8. Click the Hidden check box to hide the text.

9. Click OK to apply the formatting.

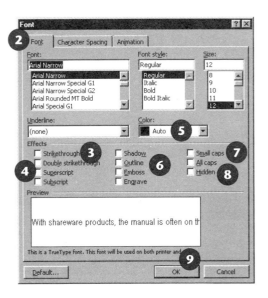

4

Formatting Paragraphs

In Word, you can specify how much space appears between each line, how the text is indented and aligned, and the position of the tab stops that line up indents and columns. Line spacing allows you to pack more information on a page with single spacing, or spread out the lines with double spacing or another value, such as 1.5-line spacing. Indent-ations and tabs can make paragraphs stand out from each other, and you can arrange information for material like tables in neat columns. To format para-graphs, you need to select the paragraphs to be formatted, and then apply one of the paragraph formatting options.

Adjust Line Spacing

① Select the paragraphs to be spaced.

② Choose Paragraph from the Format menu.

③ Click the Indents and Spacing tab, if necessary.

④ Click the Line Spacing drop-down arrow to select the spacing you want from the list.

◆ Choose Single, 1.5 Lines, or Double spacing.

◆ Choose At Least and enter a font size in the At list to specify the smallest line spacing that should be used.

◆ Choose Exactly and enter a font size in the At list to specify a fixed line spacing.

◆ Choose Multiple and enter a multiplier in the At list to specify a line spacing other than Single, Double, or 1.5 Lines.

⑤ Click OK to apply the spacing.

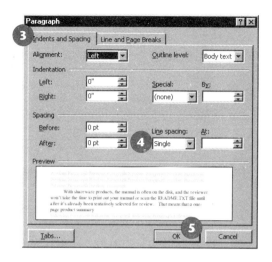

TIP

Save time spacing lines.
You can specify line spacing for the paragraph that the insertion point is in by pressing Ctrl+1 (for single spacing), Ctrl+2 (for double spacing), or Ctrl+5 (for 1.5-line spacing).

Align Text

1 Select the paragraphs you want to align.

2 Click the Align Left, Center, Align Right, or Justify buttons on the toolbar to align the text flush left/ragged right, centered, flush right/ragged left, or justified, respectively.

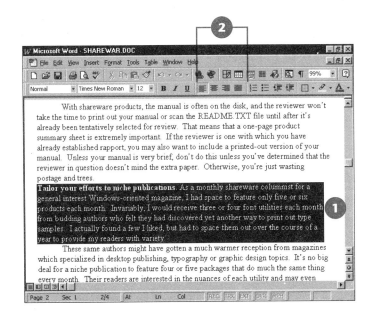

With shareware products, the manual is often on the disk, and the reviewer won't take the time to print out your manual or scan the README.TXT file until after it's already been tentatively selected for review. That means that a one-page product summary sheet is extremely important. If the reviewer is one with which you have already established rapport, you may also want to include a printed-out version of your manual. Unless your manual is very brief, don't do this unless you've determined that the reviewer in question doesn't mind the extra paper. Otherwise, you're just wasting postage and trees.

Tailor your efforts to niche publications. As a monthly shareware columnist for a general interest Windows-oriented magazine, I had space to feature only five or six products each month. Invariably, I would receive three or four font utilities each month from budding authors who felt they had discovered yet another way to print out type samples. I actually found a few I liked, but had to space them out over the course of a year to provide my readers with variety.

These same authors might have gotten a much warmer reception from magazines which specialized in desktop publishing, typography or graphic design topics. It's no big deal for a niche publication to feature four or five packages that do much the same thing every month. Their readers are interested in the nuances of each utility and may even

4

Setting Indentation and Tabs

Indentation changes the distance between the text and the side margins. Tab settings allow you to place a fixed amount of space between margins or text and other text, especially when setting up columns. Word allows you to define indents and tabs for each paragraph in a document, if you wish.

Adjust Indentation

1 Select the paragraph you want to indent.

2 Choose Paragraph from the Format menu.

3 Click the Indents And Spacing tab, if necessary.

4 Choose the amount of indentation.

- ◆ In the Left box, type the amount of indentation on the left side of all the lines in the paragraph.

- ◆ In the Right box, type the amount of indentation on the right side of all the lines in the paragraph.

- ◆ In the Special box, choose First Line or Hanging from the drop-down list, and specify an amount for a first line or hanging indent in the By box.

5 Choose the alignment (either Left, Center, Right, or Justified).

6 Click OK.

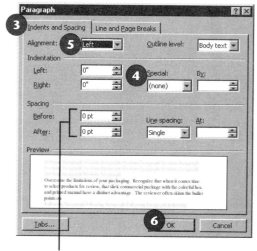

Enter values in these boxes to insert extra space before or after a paragraph.

Change tab attributes. *To specify tab positions precisely or to change the type of alignment for a tab, choose Tabs from the Format menu, select or enter the tab stop position you want to adjust, and enter the numeric values for the tab positions. You can also specify Leader Dots or Clear All Tabs in this dialog box.*

Move or delete tabs. *To move a tab, drag the Tab icon along the ruler to its new position. To delete a tab, drag the Tab icon upward or downward until it is off of the ruler.*

Add, Move, or Delete Tabs

1. Select the paragraph(s) where you want to add or modify tab stops.

2. If the Ruler is not visible at the top of your document, choose Ruler from the View menu.

3. To add a left-aligned, right-aligned, centered, or decimal tab, click the Tab icon at the far left of the ruler until the icon changes to the type of tab you want to insert.

4. Click the ruler at the position where you want to insert the tab.

4

Formatting Pages

Formatting a page allows you to apply a consistent style to the margins, headers (which appear at the top of the page), footers (which appear at the bottom of the page), and other elements of page layout. Word includes a Page Setup dialog box that allows you to quickly set margins. You can type headers and footers in the spaces provided for them at the top and bottom of each page. Word can also auto-matically insert page numbers as well as the date or time on each page in the location you specify.

Set Margins

1 Choose Page Setup from the File menu.

2 Click the Margins tab, if necessary

3 Use the arrows to specify measurements for the top, bottom, left, and right margins.

4 Use the arrows to specify measurements for header and footer from the edge of the paper.

5 Click the Apply To drop-down arrow and choose Whole Document or From This Point Forward to specify which pages the margin settings should apply to.

6 Click OK to apply the margins.

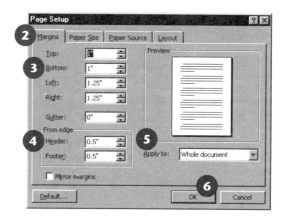

Align a header or footer.
Headers or footers can be aligned at the left or right margins or centered by selecting the header or footer and clicking the Align Left, Align Right, Center, or Justify button on the toolbar.

Use multiple-line headers or footers. *Headers or footers can consist of more than one line of text. Word expands the area at the top or bottom of the page where they are displayed if they are longer than one line.*

Add a Header and Footer

1 Choose Header And Footer from the View menu.

2 In the header or footer area, type the text you want to appear.

3 On the Header And Footer toolbar, click the Insert AutoText drop-down arrow to select the text to be automatically inserted.

4 Click the Format Page Number button on the Header And Footer toolbar.

5 Click the Close button when you are finished to apply the header or footer.

Click to show Page Setup dialog box.

Click to format page numbers.

Switch between editing the header and the footer.

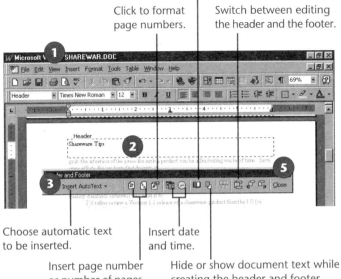

Choose automatic text to be inserted.

Insert page number or number of pages.

Insert date and time.

Hide or show document text while creating the header and footer.

4

Creating Styles

Styles are formats you can create and quickly apply to parts of paragraphs, one or more paragraphs, or entire documents. Styles can include any of the character formatting found on the Format menu, including font, font size, bold, italic, or underline characteristics. Styles can also incorporate paragraph formatting, including alignment, indentation, tabs, bullets, and numbering. You can create styles that apply to entire paragraphs, or only to selected characters. Styles can be saved in Word templates and applied anytime that template is used. New documents are always built around templates, which Word saves with a .dot filename extension. Unless you choose another template when you choose New from the File menu, Word uses Normal.dot. Templates store the toolbar settings, styles, and formatting information for your document.

Create a Paragraph Style

1. Select a paragraph you want to give the new style.

2. Use the toolbar and Format menu to apply any formatting you want to the paragraph, such as font, font size, indents, or numbering.

3. Click in the Style box on the toolbar.

4. Type the name you'd like to give the new style.

5. Press Enter when finished.

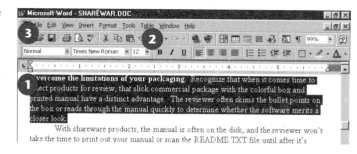

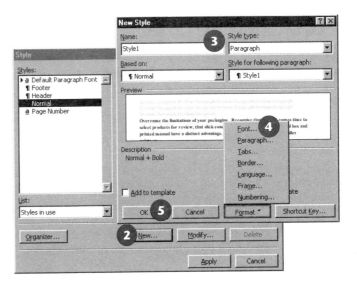

TIP

Identify paragraph styles.
Paragraph styles can be identified by the paragraph mark (¶) to the right of the style name in the Style list on the toolbar. Character styles can be identified by the underlined letter (a) that appears next to the style name in the Style list on the toolbar.

Create a Character Style

1 Choose Style from the Format menu.

2 Click the New button.

3 In the New Style dialog box:

◆ Choose Character from the Style Type drop-down list.

◆ Type a name for the new style.

◆ Click Add To Template if you want to save the new style in the current template.

4 Click the Format button, click Font, and choose the font attributes you want to apply to the style.

5 Click OK to close the New Style dialog box, and click Apply to close the Style dialog box.

4

Applying Styles

You can apply a style to a paragraph, a group of paragraphs, or to characters by selecting the text and choosing the style from the Style drop-down list on the toolbar. Different styles may be available when using different templates.

Apply a Style

1. If you want to apply a style to a single paragraph, click anywhere in it. Otherwise, select the text you want to format.

2. Click the Style drop-down arrow on the toolbar.

3. Scroll down the Style list, and click the style you want to apply.

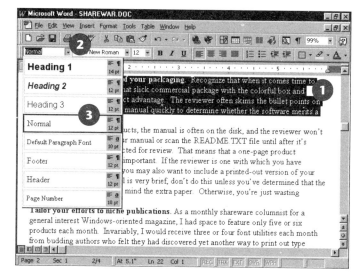

Modifying Styles

You can change any style, whether you created it or it was provided with Word, to include the formatting information you prefer. Changes you make are stored with the document's template, so you might have different style variations defined for each type of document you work with.

TIP

Remove manual formatting. *When you apply a style, it won't override any manual paragraph or character formatting that may have already been applied to the text. To remove the manual formatting before applying a style, select the entire paragraph or paragraphs. Press Ctrl+Spacebar to remove character formatting, and Ctrl+Q to remove paragraph formatting.*

Change a Style

1. Choose Style from the Format menu.

2. In the Style dialog box, choose the style you want to change from the Styles list.

3. Click the Modify button.

4. In the Modify Style dialog box, click the Format button.

5. Select the attributes you want to change, and make the modifications.

6. Click OK after changing each attribute to select another attribute to change

7. When you finish changing the style, click Add To Template if you want your changes to apply to all documents created with the current template.

8. Click OK to apply your changes to the style and return to the Style dialog box.

9. In the Style dialog box, click Close.

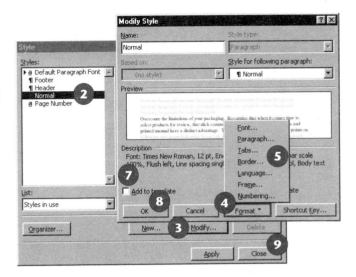

Creating Tables

Tables are an easy way to arrange information in your document in rows and columns. Word tables can be used to sort text and numbers or to perform calculations on rows and columns, just as you can with a spreadsheet. You use Word's Table toolbar button to quickly create a standard table with the number of rows and columns you want. You use the Insert Table command to specify the number of rows and columns and the width of the columns, as well as additional information. You can always add new rows or columns later, but planning a basic format first can save time.

TIP

Change a table's format.
You can change any table's format by selecting the table and then choosing Table AutoFormat from the Table menu. Then choose the new format from the scrolling list.

Create a Table by Using the Table Button

1. Click in the document where you want to insert the table.

2. Click the Insert Table button on the toolbar.

3. Drag down and to the right to specify the number of rows and columns you want.

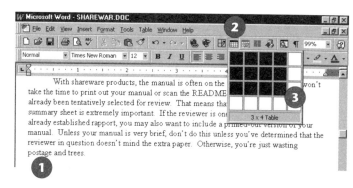

Create a Table by Using the Table Menu

1. Select Insert Table from the Table menu.

2. Click the up or down arrow to select the number of columns and rows you want.

3. Click the up or down arrow to select the column width, or choose Auto to fit the width to the column.

4. Click the AutoFormat button and choose a format from the Formats list, clicking any of the check boxes to customize the format.

5. Click OK in the Table AutoFormat and the Insert Table dialog boxes to create the table.

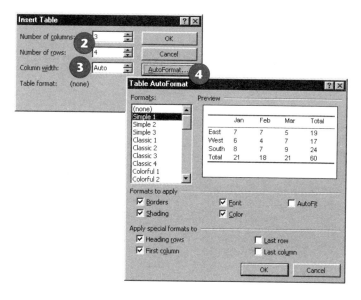

TIP

Add columns or rows. *Click in the top line of the column to the right of where you want to add a column, or click to the left of the row below where you want to add a row. Select the same number of rows or columns as the number you want to add and choose Insert Column or Insert Row from the Insert menu.*

TIP

Delete columns. *Click in the top line of the left-most column to be deleted or to the left of the top row to be deleted and drag to the right or down to select all the columns or rows you want to remove. Then choose Delete Column or Delete Row from the Insert menu.*

TIP

Move from cell to cell. *To move from cell to cell, press the Tab key to move forward (to the right), and Shift+Tab to move backward (to the left).*

Enter Text or Numbers into a Table

1 Click anywhere in the table to select it.

2 Click in any cell to enter information into it, or to change information already in it.

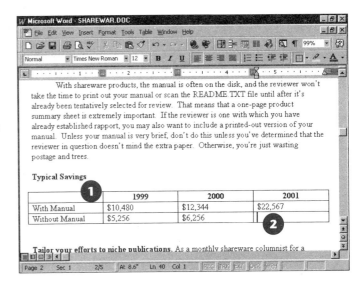

Checking Spelling

Word can improve the accuracy of your documents by searching for misspelled words, incorrect capitalization or hyphenation, and some frequent errors in composition, such as repeated words. Although Word knows the correct spelling for thousands of words, you can add words, such as specialized or technical terminology relating to your job, to a personal dictionary, so Word won't mark them as misspelled. Word can also check your grammar when it checks your spelling, or check your grammar or spelling as you type.

Check Your Spelling

1. If you don't want to check the spelling of the entire document, select just the text you want to check. Otherwise click anywhere in the document.

2. Click the Spelling And Grammar button on the toolbar.

3. Click the correct spelling on the scrolling Suggestions list, or type the correct spelling in the Not In Dictionary box.

4. Click Change to change the misspelled word to the correct spelling.

5. Click Change All to change all occurrences of the misspelled word in the current document.

6. Click Ignore to ignore the word without changing its spelling.

7. Click Ignore All to ignore every instance of the word in the document.

8. Click Add to add a correctly spelled word to your personal dictionary.

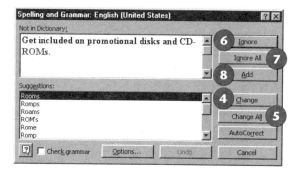

Check your grammar.
*Word can check your grammar
as you type or when you check
your spelling. Choose Options
from the Tools menu, click the
Spelling And Grammar tab,
and click the Check Grammar
With Spelling check box. To
check grammar or spelling as
you enter text, click the Check
Grammar As You Type or
Check Spelling As You Type
check boxes.*

Find a better word. *Word
can also help you locate an
alternate word for one you are
using. Select the word, and
then choose Thesaurus from
the Tools menu. A list of words
with similar meanings appears.
If you want to use the synonym
in the Replace With Synonym
box, click the Replace button.*

Add or Delete Words from Your Personal Dictionary

1 Choose Options from the Tools menu.

2 Click the Spelling And Grammar tab.

3 Click the Dictionaries button.

4 Choose the dictionary you want to edit, and click the Edit button.

5 Add, delete, or modify words in your custom dictionary.

◆ To add a list of words to the dictionary, press Enter after typing each word.

6 When you finish, save your changes by clicking the Save button on the toolbar.

7 Choose Close from the File menu to return to your document.

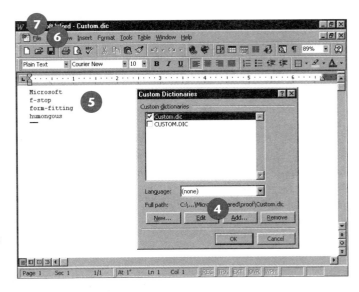

4

Formatting and Correcting Text Automatically

Word can automatically change or insert text or pictures as you type, or when you specify by using the Auto-Format command. It can format headings and bulleted and numbered lists; correct common typing, spelling, and grammatical errors; or insert standardized "boiler-plate" text when you type a few identifying characters.

Choose Automatic Correction Options

1. Choose AutoCorrect from the Tools menu.

2. Click the AutoCorrect Tab, if necessary.

3. Click the check boxes to select AutoCorrect options.

4. Click Replace Text As You Type to substitute other text for words or characters you type.

   ◆ Enter text into the Replace box.

   ◆ Enter the replacement text in the With box.

5. Click Ok.

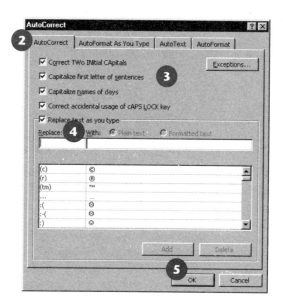

Create automatic boilerplate. *To create boiler-plate text that is inserted into your document automatically, select the text and graphics you want inserted, choose AutoCorrect from the Tools menu, click the AutoText tab, and type a shorthand name for the boilerplate. When you type that name in the future, Word will insert the text and any graphics that were in the selected text.*

Use the AutoFormat command. *Word can also apply formatting options you choose as a separate operation. Specify the options you want to use on the AutoFormat tab of the AutoCorrect dialog box. Use the AutoFormat command on the Format menu when you're ready to apply the formatting.*

Format Text Automatically

1. Choose AutoCorrect from the Tools menu.

2. Click the AutoFormat As You Type tab, if necessary.

3. Click the options for headings, borders, bulleted lists, and other choices that you want in the Apply As You Type area.

4. Click the options you want in the Replace As You Type area.

5. Click the options you want in Automatically As You Type area.

6. Click Ok.

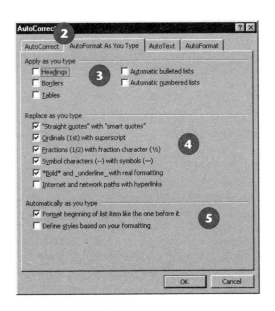

Printing Documents

Word uses the same procedures to print documents as the other Works tools, so once you've learned the method for one tool, you can apply the same method to the others. You can select a printer (if you have more than one printer connected to your computer, or your computer is on a network), preview a document to see how it will look when printed, select pages or page ranges to print, and choose from other options. If you print several copies of a document, Word can collate the pages by printing them in order multiple times.

TIP

Preview a document. *To see how a document will look before it is printed, click the Print Preview button on the toolbar.*

Print a Document

1. Choose Print from the File menu.

2. In the Print Range area, click the All option to print all of the pages in the document, or click the Pages option and enter the page range you want to print.

3. To print only one page, type the number of that page in the Pages box.

4. In the Copies area, type the number of copies you want to print.

5. Click the Collate check box if you are printing more than one copy of a document and want the pages collated.

6. Click OK to print.

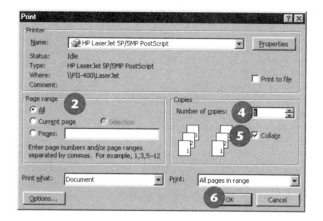

Setting Word's Optional Features

Word includes many optional features you can set to customize the way the application works for you. The most important of these include specifying how Word saves documents, and setting options for editing and general features.

Set Options

1. On the Tools menu, click Options.

2. To change general options, click the General tab.

3. To change editing options, click the Edit tab.

4. To change save options, click the Save tab.

5. Make the changes you want, and then click OK when you are finished to apply them.

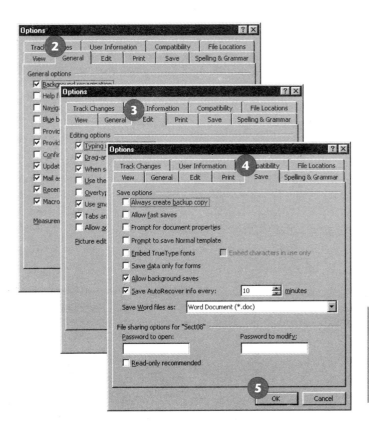

5

Calculating with Spreadsheets

While word processors popularized personal computers among those who work with words, people who need to juggle numbers have cherished spreadsheet tools. A *spreadsheet* is a kind of table that allows you to arrange figures in neat rows and columns, execute calculations, and perform "what if?" estimates simply by substituting numbers. You can use a spreadsheet's grid layout to track expenses, plan your finances, create forms like invoices, or keep simple databases of numeric information.

Spreadsheets consist of rows and columns of cells, each of which can contain text, a number, or a formula. The Works spreadsheet tool uses its own toolbar, very similar to the one found in the Works word processor tool, to help you enter, format, and calculate your information. When you've completed a spreadsheet, you can view and use it within the spreadsheet tool, or copy it into another application, such as a word processing document or even non-Works applications.

Viewing the Spreadsheet Window

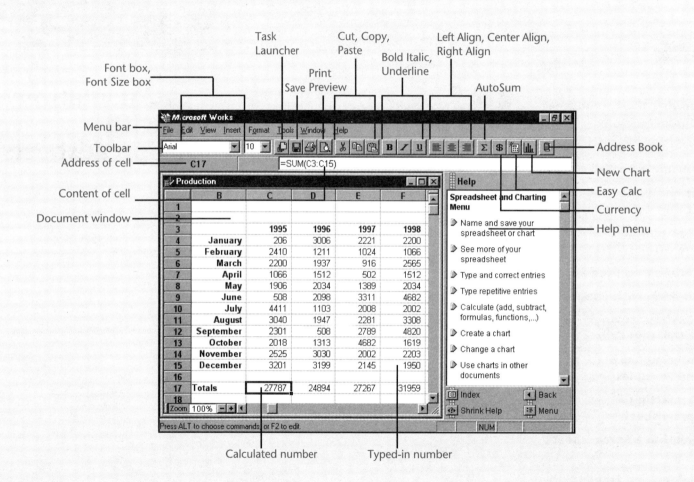

Font box,
Font Size box

Task
Launcher

Cut, Copy,
Paste

Save Print
Preview

Bold Italic,
Underline

Left Align, Center Align,
Right Align

AutoSum

Menu bar

Toolbar

Address of cell

Content of cell

Document window

Address Book

New Chart

Easy Calc

Currency

Help menu

Calculated number

Typed-in number

Creating a Spreadsheet

You can create a new Works spreadsheet the same way you create a document with the word processor or other Works tools. You can always create a blank spreadsheet no matter which Works tool you are using, and you can switch between Works tools easily. For example, if you're currently working on a word processing document and want to add a spreadsheet, you can create one and have both document windows visible on your screen at the same time. Works gives new, blank spreadsheets generic names, such as Unsaved Spreadsheet 1, which you can change to any name you like by saving the document to your hard disk drive.

Create a New Spreadsheet

1. Choose New from the File menu.

2. Click the Works Tools tab.

3. Click the Spreadsheet button.

5

Moving from Cell to Cell

Before you can enter data on your spreadsheet, you need to know how to move from one position on the spreadsheet to another. Each individual box on the spreadsheet is called a *cell*. *Rows* are made up of cells arranged horizontally. *Columns* are vertical stacks of cells, assigned letters from A to Z, and then from AA to AZ and so forth all the way to IA through IV, for a total of 256 different columns. Cells are named using addresses called *references*, which consist of their row number and column letter, starting with A1 in the upper-left corner of the spreadsheet. The fastest way to move from one cell to another is to use the arrow keys. You can also use keyboard shortcuts to move quickly. The current selected cell is called the *active cell*, and its address and contents are shown in the entry bar just below the toolbar.

Move from Cell to Cell

Press Ctrl+Home to move to cell A1.

Press the left arrow to move one column to the left.

Start here.

Press the right arrow to move one column to the right.

Press the End key to move to the last column in use in the current row.

Press the Home key to move to column A in the current row.

Press the up arrow to move one row up.

Press the down arrow to move one row down.

Press Ctrl+End to move to the last row and column in use.

Find a cell. *If you don't know the reference or address of a cell, but you know what value or formula it contains, such as "256" or "A1+B2," you can move directly to the first cell with those contents. Chose Find from the Edit menu and type the contents you want to look for. The Find dialog box has options to let you search by rows, columns, values, or formulas.*

Use scroll bars. *You can also move through a spreadsheet quickly by using the horizontal and vertical scroll bars. This technique is useful when you just want to examine, rather than work on, a portion of the spreadsheet. The active cell remains in its original location until you click a new cell.*

Move back to the active cell. *If you've scrolled until the active cell is no longer visible, you can quickly move back to it by pressing the Right arrow key followed by the Left arrow key, or the Down arrow key followed by the Up arrow key.*

Move Directly to a Cell

1 Press F5.

2 Type the cell reference.

3 Click OK.

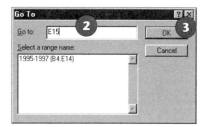

Entering Data into Cells

You can enter text, numbers, or calculations into cells. Text is most often a row or column heading, but can also be the text within a table, or just comments about your spreadsheet. Numbers are figures you type, such as the amount of money you've deposited in a savings account each month of the year. Calculations are formulas that provide a computed result. For example, you might enter a formula that adds up all your savings entries to provide a yearly total. If you begin a text entry with +, -, =, or /, Works considers it a formula and displays an error message to the right of the active cell. If Works encounters filled cells and cannot display a cell's contents to the right of the current cell, it displays an "XXXX" entry to warn you that the cell is not wide enough.

Enter Text or Numbers

1 Select the cell where you want to enter text or numbers.

2 Type the text or numbers you want to enter.

3 Press the Enter key when you finish typing the text or numbers for that cell.

Formula bar contains contents of the current cell.

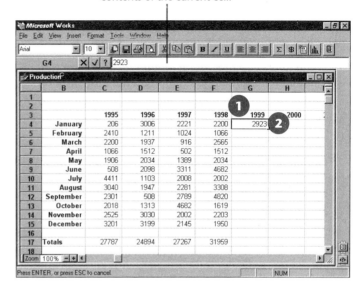

Begin text with a symbol or a number. *If you want to begin a text entry with a symbol, type a quotation mark (") as the first character in that cell so that the entry is recognized as text and not as a formula.*

Mix numbers, text, and symbols. *If you want to put only a number in a cell as text, type a quotation mark (") first, or else Works will treat it as a numeric value. However, you don't need to do this if there is text before or after the number (for example, "256 cartons" or "Ocean's 11").*

Enter Calculations

1 Select the cell where you want to enter a formula.

2 Type the formula using operators like +, -, *, or /.

3 Press the Enter key when you finish typing the formula.

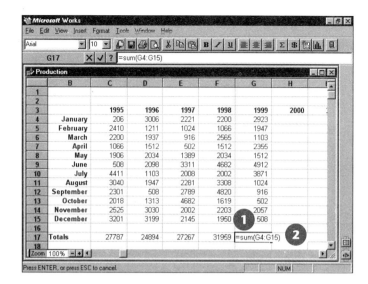

Editing Cells

You'll often want to change the contents of a cell to fix an error, or to reuse a spreadsheet for another purpose, using new figures or labels. Or you may want to perform "what if" calculations to see, for example, how much money you'd end up with if you increased the size of the monthly deposits in your savings account. Works lets you edit the contents of a cell directly, or by typing in the formula bar.

Edit Contents of a Cell Directly

1. Select the cell you want to edit.

2. Press F2 to switch to editing mode.

3. Use the mouse pointer or arrow keys to move the insertion point to the place within the cell that you want to edit.

4. Delete unwanted information using the Backspace or Delete keys, or type new information.

5. When you finish editing the cell, press Enter.

	B	C	D	E	F	G	H	
1								
2								
3		1995	1996	1997	1998	1999	2000	
4	January	206	3006	2221	2200	2923		
5	February	2410	1211	1024	1066	1947		
6	March	2200	1937	916	2565	1103		
7	April	1066	1512	502	1512			
8	May	1906	2034	1389	2034	1512		
9	June	508	2098	3311	4682	4912		
10	July	4411	1103	2008	2002	3871		
11	August	3040	1947	2281	3308	1024		
12	September	2301	508	2789	4820	916		
13	October	2018	1313	4682	1619	502		
14	November	2525	3030	2002	2203	2057		
15	December	3201	3199	2145	1950	508		
16								
17	Totals	27787	24894	27267	31959			
18								

Zoom 100%

TIP

Cancel edits. *If you change your mind about editing a cell while in editing mode, click the X in the formula bar. Works will restore your previous entry.*

Edit Contents from the Formula Bar

1. Select the cell you want to edit.

2. Place the insertion point inside the formula bar.

3. Use the mouse or arrow keys to move the insertion point to the place within the cell where you want to begin editing.

4. Delete unwanted information using the Backspace or Delete keys, or type new information.

5. When you finish editing the cell, press Enter.

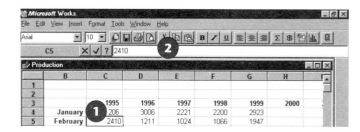

Changing Column and Row Size

Works creates rows and columns using a standard width for columns (10 characters) and standard height for rows (tall enough for the chosen font size). If you find that these sizes don't suit your needs, you can easily change them by typing new size values, by letting Works provide the best fit for your data, or by dragging the column and row borders.

Adjust Column Width or Row Height

1 Select the columns or rows you want to change.

2 Choose Column Width or Row Height from the Format menu.

   ◆ Type a value in character-widths to change the column to that width, or in points to change the row to that height.

   ◆ Click the Standard button to change the column or row to the standard width or height.

   ◆ Click the Best Fit button to change the column or row to a width or height that fits the current contents of the cell.

3 Click OK.

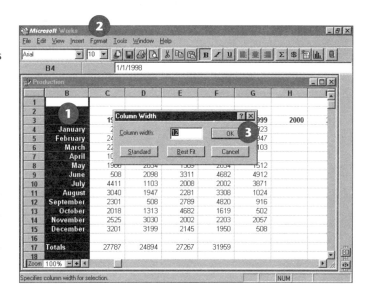

Change a column width automatically. *If you want Works to change a column's width to fit the largest entry in the column, double-click that column's header.*

Change row height. *If you want to keep the same column width but allow entries to appear on more than one line within the cell, choose Alignment from the Format menu and click the Wrap Text check box.*

Adjust Column Width and Row Height by Dragging

1. Hover the mouse pointer at the border you want to move in the row or column heading until the Adjust label appears.

2. Click and hold the mouse button to drag the row border up or down, or the column border left or right, to resize the row or column.

3. Release the mouse button when you're satisfied with the new size.

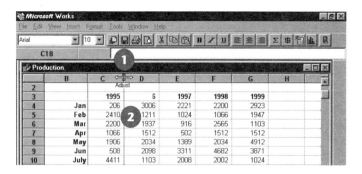

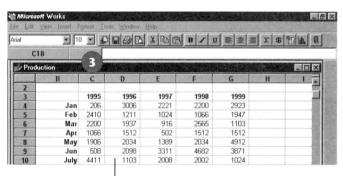

Resized column.

5

Automating Data Entry

Works can help you fill in numbers or text automatically, to save typing a repetitive series of numbers or dates, or to create row or column headers, such as a pattern of month names. Works uses the first two entries you type as a pattern, and is even smart enough to create headers like "Volume 1...Volume 2..." if you type in a pattern to follow. Works can insert numbers in forward or reverse order, such as 1, 2, 3, 4, or 10, 8, 6, 4, and can also insert dates, such as Monday, Tuesday, Wednesday, or January, February, March.

Enter a Series of Numbers Automatically

1. Type the first value in the series in a cell on the spreadsheet.

2. Type the second value in a cell in the next column or row.

3. Press the Enter key.

4. Select the two cells.

5. Hover the mouse pointer over the lower-right corner of the last cell you entered until the mouse pointer displays a Fill label under it.

6. Click and hold the mouse button and drag along the row or down the column to the last cell you want to fill automatically.

7. Release the mouse button to fill the cells.

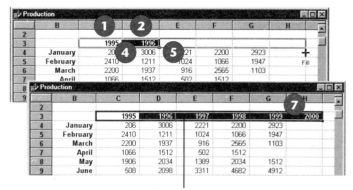

Works has filled in the series of dates.

Enter nonconsecutive numbers or dates automatically. *The pattern you set up with the first two cells does not have to be consecutive. You can type 1, 3 or 2, 4 to fill the cells with odd or even numbers, respectively, or Monday, Wednesday to fill the cells with every other day of the week.*

Use positive and negative numbers. *You can start or end a series with positive or negative numbers, or with any day of the week or month. Works adjusts to provide the correct entries. For example, starting with -8, -6 and dragging would produce the list -8, -6, -4, -2, 0, 2, 4, 6.... Starting with November would generate the list November, December, January, and so forth.*

Fill with a single value. *You can fill a row or column with a single value. Select only one cell, and drag from its lower-right corner down the row or cell in which you want the duplicates to appear.*

Enter a Series of Dates Automatically

1 Type the first date in the series in a cell on the spreadsheet.

2 Type the second date in the series in a cell in the next column or row.

3 Press the Enter key.

4 Select the two cells.

5 Hover the mouse pointer over the lower-right corner of the last cell you entered until the mouse pointer displays a Fill label under it.

6 Click and hold the mouse button and drag along the row or down the column to the last cell you want to fill automatically.

7 Release the mouse button to fill the cells.

	B	C	D	E	F	G	H
2							
3		Monday	Tuesday				
4	Week 1		3006	221	2200	2923	
5	Week 2	2410	1211	1024	1066	1947	
6	Week 3	2200	1937	916	2565	1103	
7							
8							
9							

Production

	B	C	D	E	F	G	H
2							
3		Monday	Tuesday	Wednesday	Thursday	Friday	
4	Week 1	206	3006	2221	2200	2923	
5	Week 2	2410	1211	1024	1066	1947	
6	Week 3	2200	1937	916	2565	1103	
7	Week 4	1066	1512	502	1512		
8	Week 5	1906	2034	1389	2034	1512	
9	Week 6	508	2098	3311	4682	4912	

5

Working with Ranges of Numbers

A range can consist of all or part of a row, all or part of a column, or a rectangular area consisting of both rows and columns. You can refer to a range by typing the addresses of the cells in opposite corners, separated by a colon (for example, B2:E10). You can also give a group or range of numbers on your spreadsheet a name, such as *1995-1996 Results*, and then refer to that name instead of the cell addresses when performing calculations.

Select a Range of Cells

1. Click a cell in one corner of the range you want to select.

2. Drag to the opposite corner of the range.

3. Release the mouse button.

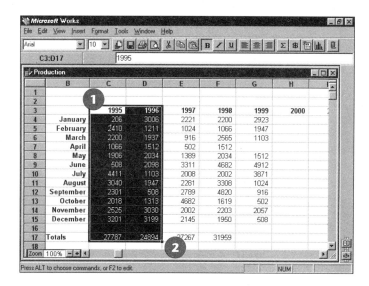

Refer to a Range by Address

1. In any dialog box or cell in which you want to reference a range of cells, type the addresses of the cells in the opposite corners of the range, separated by a colon.

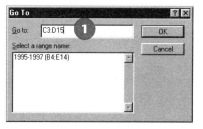

Select a range quickly.
Instead of dragging over a range, you may find it quicker to click one corner of the range, hold down the Shift key, and click the opposite corner.

Move quickly to a range.
You might not remember the cell addresses of a range, but might easily recall the range name. You can move quickly to any named range in a spreadsheet by pressing F5 and either typing the range name in the Go To box, or clicking the range name in the Select A Range Name list.

Select an entire row, column, or spreadsheet.
To select an entire row or column, click the column or row header. To select the entire spreadsheet, click the unlabeled box in the top-left corner where the column and row headers meet.

Assign a Name to a Range of Cells

1 Select the range of cells you want to name.

2 Choose Range Name from the Insert menu.

3 Type a name in the Name box.

4 Click OK to apply the name to the range.

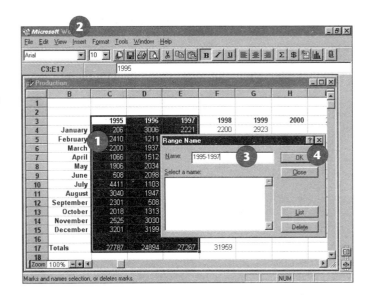

Copying, Moving, or Deleting Cells

Works provides several ways to copy, move, or delete cells on a spreadsheet. You can perform these tasks using the same Copy, Cut, and Paste buttons you use in the word processor tool. Using these toolbar buttons is the best choice when copying or moving cells over large distances on the spreadsheet. If you want to move or copy the cells only a short distance, you can drag them using the mouse.

Copy a Cell or Range

1. Select the cell or range to be copied.

2. Click the Copy button on the toolbar.

3. Click the location in the spreadsheet where you want to insert the cells.

4. Click the Paste button on the toolbar.

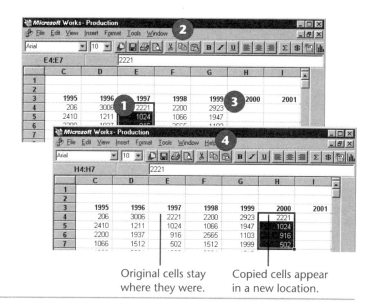

Original cells stay where they were.

Copied cells appear in a new location.

Move or Delete a Cell or Range

1. Select the cell or range to be moved or deleted.

2. Click the Cut button on the toolbar to delete the cells from the spreadsheet.

3. If you want to place the removed cells somewhere else, click the new location.

4. Click the Paste button on the toolbar.

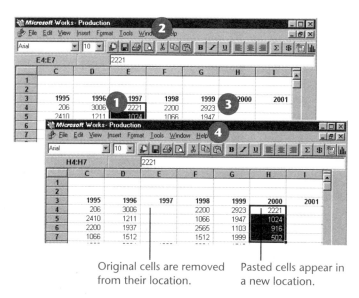

Original cells are removed from their location.

Pasted cells appear in a new location.

Copy or Move by Dragging

1 Select the cell or range to be copied or moved.

2 Move the mouse pointer to the border surrounding the cell or range until the Drag label appears under it.

3 Move the cell or range by dragging the cell or range to a new location, or copy the cell or range by holding down the Ctrl key as you drag.

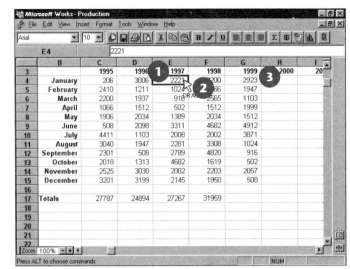

Calculating Numbers Automatically

Works includes a feature that can help you create and insert formulas on your spreadsheet automatically. You just select the cell into which you want to put the calculation and click the EasyCalc button. The EasyCalc dialog box allows you to choose from addition, subtraction, multiplication, division, averages, and other calculations. You can even include advanced mathematical, financial, statistical, or date and time calculations without needing to know the formulas themselves.

Insert a Formula Automatically

1. Select the cell where you want to insert the formula.

2. Click the EasyCalc button.

3. Click the button representing the kind of formula you want to create.

4. Click the first cell the formula will be applied to, and then click the last cell.

5. Click the Next button.

6. Click the Next button to accept the suggested position for the results. You can also type the cell address where the results should appear.

7. If data is already contained in the cell where the formula will appear, Works will ask you to confirm that you want to replace that information by clicking OK.

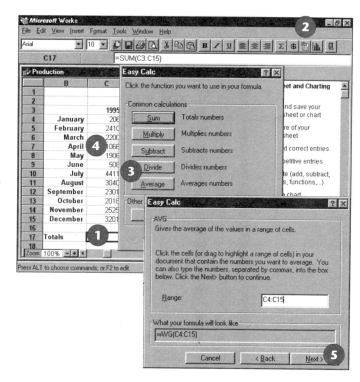

SEE ALSO

For information on creating your own formulas, see "Writing a Formula" on page 86.

TIP

Calculate financial items.
Works' built-in financial formulas make it easy to create a budget or calculate interest rates on loans and savings.

Insert an Advanced Formula

1. Click the cell where you want to insert the formula.

2. Click the EasyCalc button.

3. Click the Other button.

4. Choose the type of formula you want to use from the Category list.

5. Select the function from the Choose A Function list.

6. Click the Insert button to insert the formula.

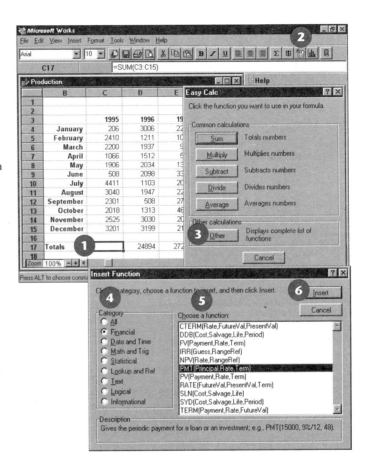

Writing a Formula

If you type a formula in a cell, Works calculates a result and displays it in the cell. A formula can be as simple as the sum of a range of cells in a row or column, or it can perform several different calculations on more than one range, or even on numbers that you type in a cell.

TIP

Automatically sum a row or column. *To quickly add up a row or column, choose an empty cell at the end of the row or column, click the Auto-Sum button on the toolbar, and press Enter.*

Create a Formula

1. Click the cell where you want to enter the formula.

2. Type an equal sign (=) to indicate that you are typing a formula, and then type a mathematical expression using numbers, cell addresses, ranges or range names, and mathematical operators.

3. Press Enter when you finish.

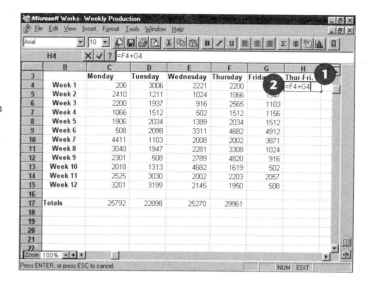

TO INSERT A FORMULA		
To	**Do this**	**Example**
Perform math operations on cells	Type cell addresses separated by math operators such as + or -.	=A1+A2; =A1+A2-(C2+C4); =E4-E2*D2; =E15/E14,
Perform math operations on numbers	Type the numbers in the cell using math operators.	5.25+6.42; 5*8*2; (15+2)-(3+4)*8
Add the contents of a row or column	Type **SUM**, followed by the range of addresses or range name in parentheses.	=SUM(E4:E8); =SUM (C1:F1)

Copy the results of a formula. *If you copy a cell containing a formula, Works makes a copy of the formula itself, rather than the current results. If you want to copy the results, select the cell, click the Copy button on the toolbar, click the cell where you want to paste the results, choose Paste Special from the Edit menu, and then click Add Values and click OK.*

Clear a formula. *To remove a formula, click the cell containing the formula and press the Backspace key.*

View formulas. *To have Works display formulas rather than the results calculated from those formulas, choose Formulas from the View menu.*

Insert a Cell or Range Reference into a Formula

1. Type an equal sign in the cell where you want to begin the formula, and then type the formula up to the point where the cell or range reference should go.

2. Select the cell or range to be inserted into the formula.

3. After Works inserts the range reference you selected, type the rest of the formula.

4. Press the Enter key.

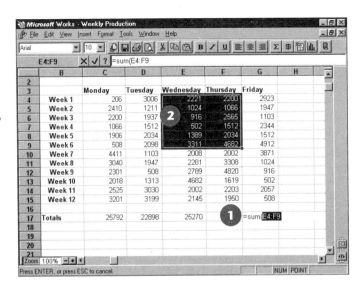

Formatting a Spreadsheet

You can format a spreadsheet to improve its appearance, to give row or column headers a distinct appearance, or to assign specific number or text formats to cells or ranges. For example, you can use a larger font for headers or use a different font for text entries. A spreadsheet can be formatted manually or utomatically.

Format Selected Rows and Columns

1. Select the rows or columns to be formatted.

2. From the Format menu, choose the attribute you want to apply.

   ◆ Click the Number tab to specify the number of decimal places, the use of a dollar sign for currency, to format a number as a date, time, fraction, or other numeric formats.

   ◆ Click the Alignment tab to specify horizontal or vertical alignment, text wrapping at the ends of lines, and other options.

   ◆ Click the Border Or Shading tab to add borders or shading to cells.

3. Click OK to apply the formatting.

4. With the rows or columns still selected, apply font, font size, and attributes such as bold, italic, or underline from the toolbar.

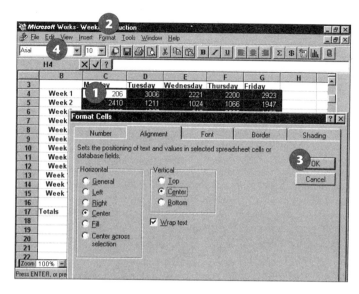

TIP

Format cells for dollars and cents. *To quickly format a cell or range of cells for dollars and cents, select the cells you want to format, and click the Currency button on the toolbar.*

TIP

Provide automatic totals. *If you're formatting cells automatically, click the Format Last Row And/Or Column As Total check box and Works will insert a formula in the last row or column summing that row or column.*

Format a Spreadsheet Automatically

1 Select the cell or range you want to format.

2 Choose AutoFormat from the Format menu.

3 Choose a format from the Select A Format list.

4 After reviewing the sample shown in the Example window, click OK to apply the format.

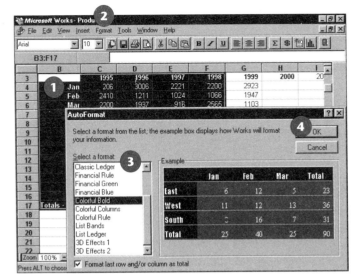

Creating a Spreadsheet Chart

Works can convert your spreadsheet information into a chart. Charts can help you examine numeric information visually in a way that is easier to understand than in a table or spreadsheet. Once you've created a chart from a spreadsheet, each time you update the spreadsheet, the chart will be modified as well.

Create a Chart

1. Select the range of cells to be plotted in the chart.

2. Click the Chart button on the toolbar.

3. Choose a chart type.

4. Type a title for the chart in the Title box.

5. Click OK to create the chart.

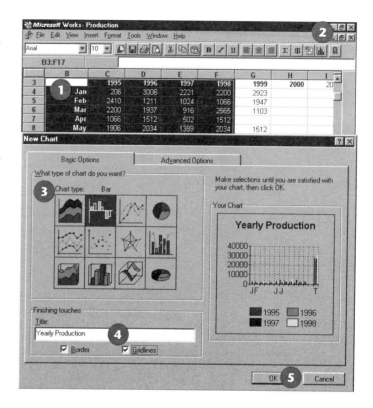

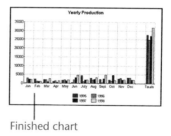

Finished chart

TIP

Create multiple charts.
Each spreadsheet can contain up to eight different charts. If you need to make additional charts from the same data, copy or link the data to a new spreadsheet.

TIP

Organize for easy charting.
If the first row or column of the range you've selected contains numbers, Works includes them in the charted data. If the first row or column contains text, dates, or times, Works uses them as labels.

Modify a Chart Type

1. Select the chart you want to change.

2. On the toolbar, click the button for the new type of chart you want.

3. Click the Variations tab in the Chart Type dialog box to choose one of the different varieties of that chart.

4. Click OK to apply the changes.

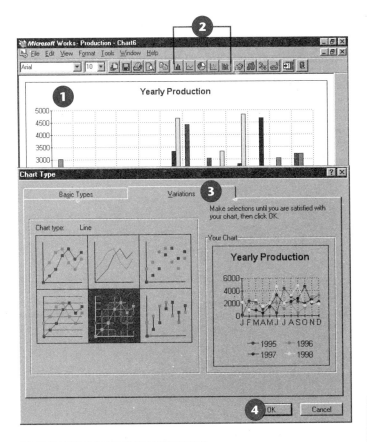

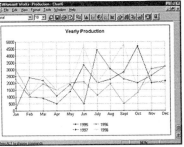

Linking and Embedding Files

Works allows you to share information between documents using *linking* or *embedding*. When information is linked, whenever the data in the original file is modified, the copy in the linked document is updated. When data is embedded in a document, the information is not linked to the original source information, but to the application that created it. If you embed a spreadsheet in a word processing document, you can edit the spreadsheet using the spreadsheet's tools while still using the word processing tool. However, if you update the original source information in the document you copied the data from, the embedded information is not updated in the destination document you copied it to.

Link Information Between Works Applications

1 Open the spreadsheet that is the source for the information to be linked.

2 Select the range to link.

3 Choose Range Name from the Insert menu. Type the name in the Name box or choose it from the Select A Name list, and click OK.

4 Open the destination document in which you want to insert the data.

5 Click where you want to insert the information.

6 Choose Spreadsheet from the Insert menu.

7 Click the Use A Range From An Existing Spreadsheet option button.

8 Click the name of the spreadsheet in the list of open spreadsheets.

9 Click a named range on the Select A Range list.

10 Click OK to insert and link the information.

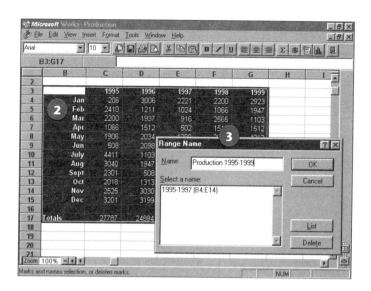

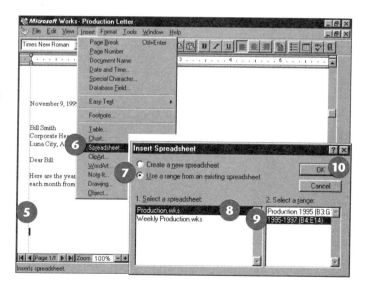

SEE ALSO

For information on the difference between linking and embedding, see "Knowing When to Link or Embed" on page 94.

TIP

Link a chart. *Instead of linking spreadsheet cells in another Works document, insert a chart. Select a position in the destination document, choose Chart from the Insert menu, click Existing Chart, choose the spreadsheet the chart was based on, and click the name of the existing chart you want to link to the current document.*

TRY THIS

Link an entire file. *To link, rather than embed, an entire file, follow the instructions for embedding an entire file, but click the Link check box before clicking the OK button.*

Embed an Existing File

1 Close the file that will be embedded, if necessary.

2 Open the document in which you want to add an object.

3 Click where you want the object to be embedded.

4 Choose Object from the Insert menu.

5 Click the Create From File option button.

6 Click the Browse button and select the file you want to embed.

7 Click Insert.

8 Click the OK button to embed the file in the destination document.

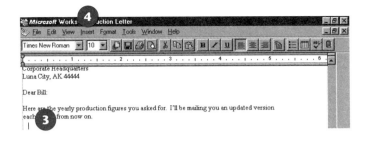

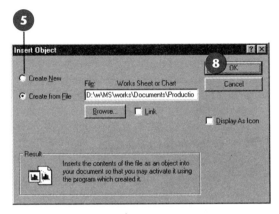

Knowing When to Link or Embed

Linking allows you to use consistently updated versions of text, spreadsheet cells, graphics, or other objects in many different documents. For example, you can link a chart with the original spreadsheet cells used to create the chart. As the spreadsheet is revised, the chart document is also updated. Each time the original document is revised, all linked versions are also updated. However, the reverse is true: to edit the linked information in any document, you must return to the original file where the information originated, and edit it there.

Embedding places a copy of the information or file in your document. The copy becomes an independent version of the original information; editing the data in the original application has no effect on the copied version in the additional document. However, you can make any edits to the copied data in the new document without opening the original application. For example, you can edit a word processing document placed in a spreadsheet, or a spreadsheet embedded in a word processing document without switching to the other tool.

To decide whether to link or embed, look at how the document will be used. If you want to insert a range from a spreadsheet in a report or other document, and have that information updated consistently, use linking. You might also use linking to place a graphic such as a logo in a document. Any time the logo is changed, the modified version will automatically appear in any linked documents.

If, on the other hand, you have information such as text, a spreadsheet, or a graphic that changes often within a document, use embedding so you can edit the object directly. You can link or embed information between many different Works and non-Works applications.

6

Tracking Information with Databases

Databases are collections of information arranged so you can quickly find and sort the information, search through the data by attributes that are of interest to you, and arrange it into reports that summarize the contents of the database in useful ways. A database is a great way to keep track of names and addresses, inventories, music or stamp collections, club membership lists, and other sets of information. Works' database capabilities make it easy to create these kinds of compilations of information. You can type information either into a spreadsheet-like table of rows and columns or into custom-designed forms. Then when you've finished collecting your data, you can sort it, look for records that match criteria you choose, and issue reports summarizing the results. The larger your collection of information, the more you need to manage it using a Works database.

About Databases

Databases are often compared with collections of index cards, because they consist of separate records that correspond to individual index cards, and categories of information that are the same for each card, much like an index card collection of recipes. So, each *record* in a database is an assemblage of information about one person, inventory item, CD recording, recipe, or other item. Within the record are the individual pieces of information, such as a name, phone number, product code, recording artist, or recipe ingredient.

In a database, these different pieces are called *fields*. If you'd rather visualize a database as a table or spreadsheet, a record might consist of an entire row, with fields defined for each column in the row. In fact, Works lets you view your database either as a table list that looks like a spreadsheet or as a form that resembles a large index card.

Works databases can include your own customized fields that are defined to best suit your own collections of data. Once you've created a database, you can sort records alphabetically or numerically, filter them to find only records that meet specific search criteria, or create reports that list all the records sorted and grouped in the way you'd like.

Viewing the Database Window

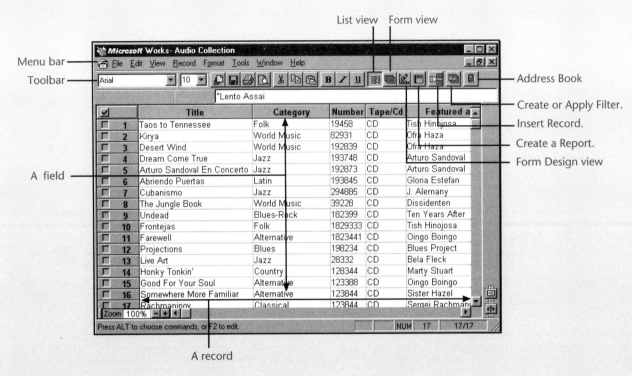

List view · Form view

Menu bar

Toolbar

A field

A record

Address Book

Create or Apply Filter.

Insert Record.

Create a Report.

Form Design view

		Title	Category	Number	Tape/Cd	Featured a
	1	Taos to Tennessee	Folk	19458	CD	Tish Hinojosa
	2	Kirya	World Music	82931	CD	Ofra Haza
	3	Desert Wind	World Music	192839	CD	Ofra Haza
	4	Dream Come True	Jazz	193748	CD	Arturo Sandoval
	5	Arturo Sandoval En Concerto	Jazz	192873	CD	Arturo Sandoval
	6	Abriendo Puertas	Latin	193845	CD	Gloria Estefan
	7	Cubanismo	Jazz	294885	CD	J. Alemany
	8	The Jungle Book	World Music	39228	CD	Dissidenten
	9	Undead	Blues-Rock	182399	CD	Ten Years After
	10	Frontejas	Folk	1829333	CD	Tish Hinojosa
	11	Farewell	Alternative	1823441	CD	Oingo Boingo
	12	Projections	Blues	198234	CD	Blues Project
	13	Live Art	Jazz	28332	CD	Bela Fleck
	14	Honky Tonkin'	Country	128344	CD	Marty Stuart
	15	Good For Your Soul	Alternative	123388	CD	Oingo Boingo
	16	Somewhere More Familiar	Alternative	123844	CD	Sister Hazel
	17	Rachmaninov	Classical	123844	CD	Sergei Rachman

Microsoft Works- Audio Collection

File   Edit   View   Record   Format   Tools   Window   Help

Arial   10   "Lento Assai

Zoom 100%

Press ALT to choose commands, or F2 to edit.   NUM   17   17/17

6

Creating a Database

Before you can enter information into a database, you must first create the form for the database. It's a good idea to think about what fields you want to include in your database and how you'd like them formatted. Every category that you might want to search for later should be given its own field. For example, if you decide a collectibles database should include fields for the name of the item, its manufacturer, the date it was made, and the price, you'll want to format the name and manufacturer fields as text, the date as either a date field or number field, and the price using dollars-and-cents formatting.

Create a Database

1 Choose New from the File menu.

2 Click the Works Tools tab.

3 Click the Database button.

4 Type the name of the first field you want to appear.

5 In the Format area, click an option button to indicate the type of field you want, such as General, Number, Date, Time, Text, and so forth.

◆ Choose the General format to align text to the left and numbers to the right.

◆ Choose Text for entries containing text, or for numeric entries that you want treated as text, such as phone numbers or postal codes.

6 If you chose a format other than General or Text, select the options you want from the Appearance list.

◆ For numbers, you can choose the number of digits, number of digits to the right of the decimal point, whether you want a dollar sign to precede the number, and other options.

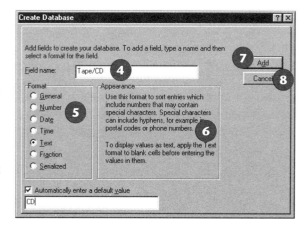

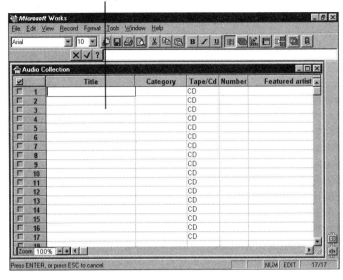
Finished empty database

Place a default value in a field. *If you want Works to insert a standard value in a field (such as $0.00 in a number field), click the Automatically Enter A Default Value check box, and type the value you want to use. This option is available for all field formats except Serialized.*

Use long field names. *Each field name can be up to 15 characters. Works widens the column in List view to accommodate longer names up to the limit.*

Insert a field. *To add a field after a database has been created, right-click the field name that you want to add a field before or after. Point to Insert Field on the shortcut menu that appears, and choose Before or After.*

◆ For date fields, you can choose a format for the date, such as 03/99, March 1999, or another combination.

◆ For time fields, you can specify whether a 12-hour or 24-hour clock is used and whether seconds are shown.

◆ For fraction fields, you can indicate how values to the right of the decimal point should be expressed in fractions. Click the Do Not Reduce check box if you want the fractions expressed as written.

◆ For serialized fields, used to number records, you can enter the next number to be used and how many to add for each new entry.

7 Click Add to add the field to your database.

8 When you've added all the fields you want to your database, click Done.

6

Filling Out a Database

Once a database is created, you can enter records in it by typing information into each of the fields. Not all the fields must be filled in, but until you add the information, you will be unable to search or sort that record by the empty field. You can enter information either in List view, which displays your database in a spreadsheet-like format with rows and columns, or in Form view, which displays each record and its fields shown together on a separate page. Using List view is a good method for entering data that already is in tabular form, while Form view is preferable when each record is a separate item or document.

Fill Fields in List View

1 Click the List View button on the toolbar.

2 Click the field you'd like to fill in.

3 Type the information.

4 Press Tab to move to the next field, or Shift+Tab to move to the preceding field.

5 When you're finished entering information, click the Save button to save the database to your hard disk drive.

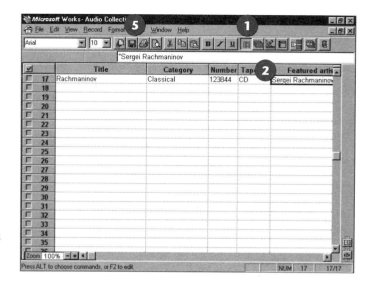

TIP

Move quickly through the database. *Use the Down arrow and Up arrow keys to move from one record to another within the same field.*

SEE ALSO

For more information on creating forms, see "Designing a Form" on page 108.

Fill Fields in Form View

1. Click the Form View button on the toolbar.

2. Click the field you'd like to fill in.

3. Type the information.

4. Press Tab or the Down arrow key to move to the next field, or Shift+Tab or the Up arrow key to move to the preceding field.

5. When you're finished entering information, click the Save button to save the database to your hard disk drive.

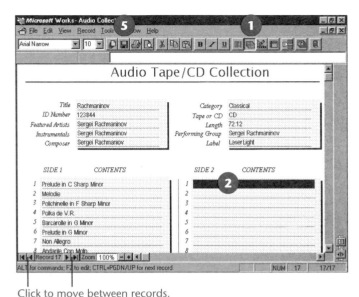

Click to move between records.

Adding or Deleting Records

Once you've entered information into your database, you'll want to add or remove records from time to time to keep it up to date. You can add records in either List view or Form view, but it's easier to remove records using List view.

Add a New Record

1. Click either the List View or the Form View button.

2. If you're in List view, press Ctrl+End, followed by Tab to move to the first field of the new record. If you're using Form view, just press Ctrl+End to create a new record.

3. Add your data.

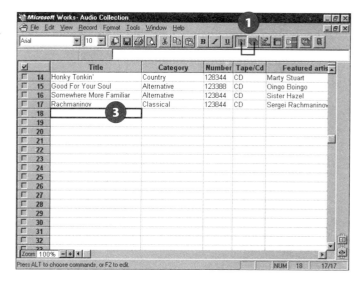

Insert a record within a database. *If you'd rather insert a record into a specific position in your database instead of at the end, click in the position where you'd like to add the record in either List view or Form view, and then choose Insert Record from the Record menu.*

Renumber records. *When you insert or delete a record, Works renumbers all of the other records.*

Delete a Record

1. Click the List View button.

2. Select the records you'd like to remove.

3. Choose Delete Record from the Record menu.

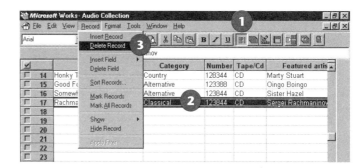

6

Copying, Deleting, and Moving Data

You can copy, delete, and move data from one record to another. You might want to copy data to duplicate records that contain the same information, or delete data in some fields in the record without changing other fields. You can move data from one record to another if you decide it belongs in a new location.

TIP

Move by dragging. *If you're copying or moving data only a short distance, using Works' drag-and-drop features may be faster. Select the data you want to move, and hold the mouse pointer in the lower-right corner until the mouse pointer has a Drag label underneath it. Then drag the data to its new location. If you hold down the Ctrl key while you drag, the data will be copied instead of moved.*

Copy, Delete, or Move Data

1 Click the List View button.

2 Select the fields you want to copy, delete, or move.

3 Click the Copy button on the toolbar if you want to copy the data, or click the Cut button if you want to delete or move the data.

4 If you are copying or moving information, click in the new location.

5 Click the Paste button on the toolbar.

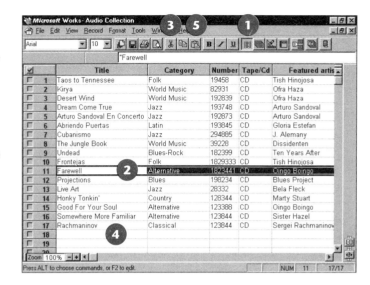

Editing Data and Field Names

You may need to change the name of fields to reflect changes in the way you'd like to keep your records. For example, if you've converted your music collection from one medium to another, you might want to change the name of a field from Record Albums to Audio CDs. You can also modify the contents of a field at any time.

TIP

Change several records quickly. *If you need to make changes in similar fields for several different records, using List view is faster. If you plan to make changes in a variety of fields in several different records, Form view provides faster access.*

SEE ALSO

For information on changing field names on a form, see "Designing a Form" on page 108.

Change Field Contents

1. Click either the List View or the Form View button.

2. Find the record containing the field you want to change.

3. Click the field to be changed.

4. Type the replacement information.

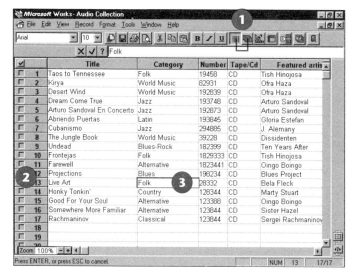

Change a Field Name or a Field's Format

1. Click the List View button on the toolbar.

2. Click anywhere in the column containing the field you want to edit.

3. Choose Field from the Format menu.

4. Type a new name for the field, or make changes in format or appearance.

5. Click OK.

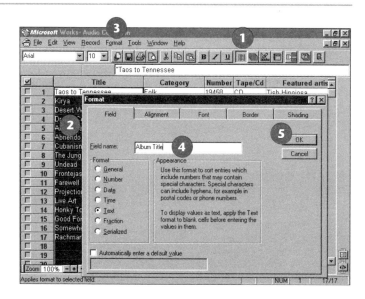

6

Changing Field and Row Size and Position

You can modify the size and position of fields and rows so they better suit the way you'd like to store your records. For example, you might want to widen a field to make it more prominent, or have several fields grouped together that are now separated in the database display. Keep in mind that when you move a field, you're moving a whole column, and not just a field within a single record.

Move a Field

1 Click the List View button on the toolbar.

2 Click the header at the top of the field you want to move.

3 Drag the field to the right or left to its new position.

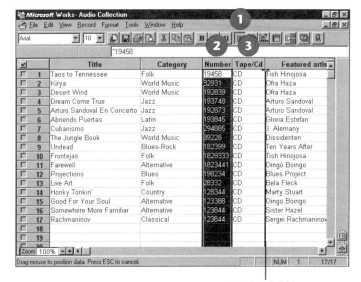

Position field is being moved to.

Move a record. *Entire rows can't be moved by dragging. Instead, use Form view, locate the record you want to move, and then select Cut Record from the Edit menu. Move to the new location, then choose Paste Record from the Edit menu.*

Resize a field precisely. *To change a field width to an exact value, choose Field Width from the Format menu and type the character width that you want the field to be.*

Choose "best fit" width quickly. *Works can adjust the field width to fit the widest entry. Just double-click the field header.*

Resize a Field or Row

1. Click the List View button on the toolbar.

2. Hover the mouse pointer over the right or left border in the header at the top of a field, or the top or bottom border of the header of the row you want to resize, until the Adjust label appears.

3. Drag the border left or right to resize the field or up or down to resize a row.

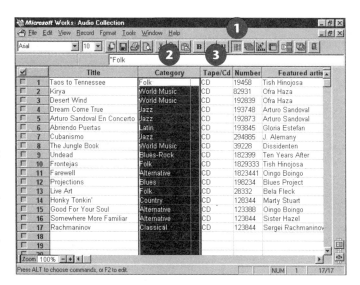

Designing a Form

If you want to create a custom form, such as a job application, Form Design view lets you lay out a form, arrange the entry fields any way you'd like, and add enhanced features such as borders, patterns, or colors. Because forms are an easier way of collecting data, if you like, you can print out your new form and use it to collect data manually that will later be keyed into your database. Even if you design a fancy form, Works still can show your records in a plain vanilla line-by-line format in List view.

Design a Form

1. In a new, empty database, click the Form Design button on the toolbar.

2. Make changes to the form. If you wish, click any of the field names you defined when you created the database and type new names for any of the fields.

   ◆ Drag the field entry box to change its size.

   ◆ Drag the field around on the form to position it as you'd like.

   ◆ Right-click any of the elements on the form and choose the Alignment, Font And Style, Border, or Shading commands for that element from the shortcut menu that appears.

   ◆ Right-click in an empty area of the form and choose to insert a field, label, or rectangle from the shortcut menu that appears.

Drag to change size. Drag to a new location.

Select command from shortcut menu.

Searching for Information

Works' Find feature can help you find a specific record within your database. You can type a word, phrase, number, or only partial information, such as "Taos" if you know the record contains that word, but aren't certain of the rest, Works can find the next match in your database or locate all the records that satisfy the search criteria.

Create a Search

1 Click the List View button.

2 Press Ctrl+Home to move to the beginning of the database.

3 Choose Find from the Edit menu.

4 Enter the word, phrase, or number you're searching for.

5 Click the OK button.

Works highlights a field it locates.

6

Sorting and Filtering Databases

One of the easiest ways to view data in an organized way is to sort it either alphabetically or numerically, or to filter the data so only records that meet criteria you specify are shown. You can sort by any of the fields in your database, and specify second or third fields to sort by to differentiate records with the same entry in the first field. Filters are reusable sets of criteria that you can apply to the database any time you want, picking only those records that match your search requirements. You can search an address list for only entries from a particular city or state—or both—using comparisons such as *is equal to, begins with*, or other comparisons.

Sort a Database

1. Click the List View button.

2. Choose Sort Records from the Record menu.

3. In the Sort Records dialog box, click the first field to sort by in the drop-down list.

4. Click either the Ascending or Descending option button to specify the order of the records.

5. If you want to further sort records, choose Ascending or Descending order.

6. Click OK.

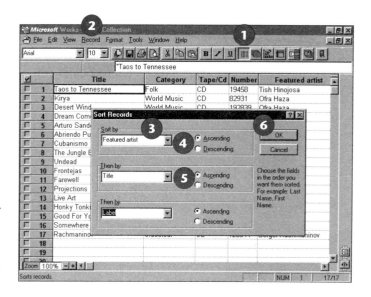

Use opposite criteria. *If you'd like to search only for the records that do not meet the filter's criteria, click the Invert Filter check box and click Apply.*

Filter a Database

1. Click the Filters button on the toolbar.

2. If you have already created a filter for this database, click the New Filter button to open the Filter Name dialog box.

3. Enter a name for the filter.

4. In the Field Name column, click the name of the field you want to compare in the drop-down list.

5. In the Comparison column, click the comparison you want to make in the drop-down list.

6. Enter the information to search for in the Compare To box.

7. If you'd like to filter using additional criteria, click And or Or in the first box at the beginning of the other comparison lines, and enter comparison information as in steps 4 and 5.

8. Click the Close button to save the filter for use later, or click the Apply Filter button to search through the database now.

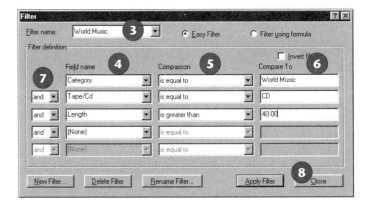

Creating Reports

Creating a report is a way to collect information from your database and print it as a hardcopy for your review. You might want to create a report showing the quantities of products in your inventory, or the number of jazz CDs in your collection. Once you've created a report format, you can use it over and over.

Create a Report

1 Choose ReportCreator from the Tools menu.

2 Type a name for the report in the Report Name dialog box and click OK.

3 Define your report in the ReportCreator dialog box.

◆ On the Title tab, revise the name of the report, choose orientation, and select a font and font size.

◆ On the Fields tab, specify which fields in your database should appear in the report.

◆ On the Sorting tab, choose up to three fields to sort the report by, and either ascending or descending order.

◆ On the Filter tab, create or select filters to be used to choose records for the report.

◆ On the Grouping tab, assemble records that have the same values in one of the fields.

4 Click the Done button when you finish to see a preview from which you can print the report or modify it.

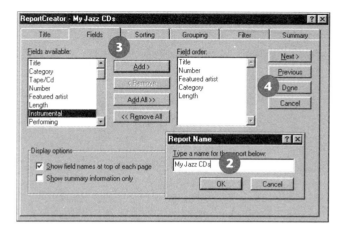

Hide records. *You can hide records from view. In List view, select the records you want to hide, and then choose Hide Records from the Records menu.*

Change a view without filters. *If you don't want to use a filter, you can still choose to show only current, unhidden records in the database, or all records including those that have been hidden. Just choose either option from the Select A Filter list on the Filter tab of the ReportCreator dialog box.*

Modify a Report

1 To change the sorting method for a report, choose Report Sorting from the Tools menu.

2 To change the groupings for a report, choose Report Grouping from the Tools menu.

3 To change the filtering methods for a report, choose Report Filtering from the Tools menu.

Using Works Databases with Other Applications

Databases you create with Microsoft Works can easily be shared with other applications, such as earlier versions of Works, or programs that use dBase III or dBase IV file formats. Most database and spreadsheet programs, such as Microsoft Access and Microsoft Excel, can also work with fields that have been saved as text separated by commas or tabs. Saving in an alternate file format is called *exporting*. If you want to share your Works databases with friends or colleagues, you can choose one of these optional file formats when you use the Save As command to create a copy of your file.

Export a Works Database File

1. Choose Save As from the File menu.

2. Choose the file format you want from the Save As Type drop-down list.

3. Click the Save button.

Managing Events and Appointments with Works Calendar

Microsoft Works Calendar is a terrific stand-alone tool. It must be started separately, rather than from within the main Works application. You can use Calendar for managing your time and appointments. You can create a calendar for your personal use, or combine all your family's activities into a single schedule. You can enter an appointment that will happen on a single day or time, as well as recurring appointments that occur at the same time every day, week, month, or year. Events can carry over to subsequent years, too. Set an anniversary or other important date once, and never worry about forgetting it again. Appointments can be categorized, so you can view all your family's medical appointments or other type of event at a glance. Works Calendar can notify you of an upcoming appointment a week ahead of time, or as little as 30 minutes before it takes place, whichever you prefer. You can even share your appointment information with others by e-mail, HTML pages, or other options.

Viewing the Calendar Window

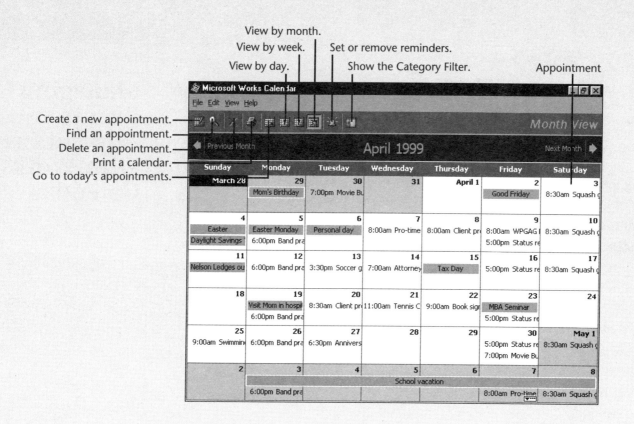

View by month.

View by week.

View by day.

Set or remove reminders.

Show the Category Filter.

Appointment

Create a new appointment.

Find an appointment.

Delete an appointment.

Print a calendar.

Go to today's appointments.

Microsoft Works Calendar

File Edit View Help

Month View

Previous Month

April 1999

Next Month

Sunday	Monday	Tuesday	Wednesday	Thursday	Friday	Saturday
March 28	29 Mom's Birthday	30 7:00pm Movie Bu	31	April 1	2 Good Friday	3 8:30am Squash
4 Easter Daylight Savings	5 Easter Monday 6:00pm Band pra	6 Personal day	7 8:00am Pro-time	8 8:00am Client pr	9 8:00am WPGAG 5:00pm Status re	10 8:30am Squash
11 Nelson Ledges ou	12 6:00pm Band pra	13 3:30pm Soccer g	14 7:00am Attorney	15 Tax Day	16 5:00pm Status re	17 8:30am Squash
18	19 Visit Mom in hospi 6:00pm Band pra	20 8:30am Client pr	21 11:00am Tennis C	22 9:00am Book sign	23 MBA Seminar 5:00pm Status re	24
25 9:00am Swimmin	26 6:00pm Band pra	27 6:30pm Annivers	28	29	30 5:00pm Status re 7:00pm Movie Bu	May 1 8:30am Squash
2	3 6:00pm Band pra	4	5 School vacation	6	7 8:00am Pro-time	8 8:30am Squash

Changing Calendar Views

If your schedule is busy, you can examine your calendar from a view that shows one day's appointments at a time. You can also view the calendar from a weekly or monthly perspective to examine the "big picture." In any view, you can scroll to the next or previous day, week, or month by clicking the navigation arrows just below the toolbar.

TIP

Change the starting day of the week. *Choose Options from the View menu, and you can select a default starting day of the week other than Sunday. You can also choose the first hour of the day that appears on a calendar entry, from the default time of 7 A.M. to any time you want.*

View by Day, Week, or Month

1. To view a day's events, click the View Day button.

2. To see a week's worth of events, click the View Week button.

3. To see the current month's events, click the View Month button.

4. To jump quickly to today's appointments whether you're using Day, Week, or Month view, click the Go To Today button on the toolbar.

5. To scroll to the next or previous day, week, or month's appointments, click the right and left navigation arrows located below the toolbar.

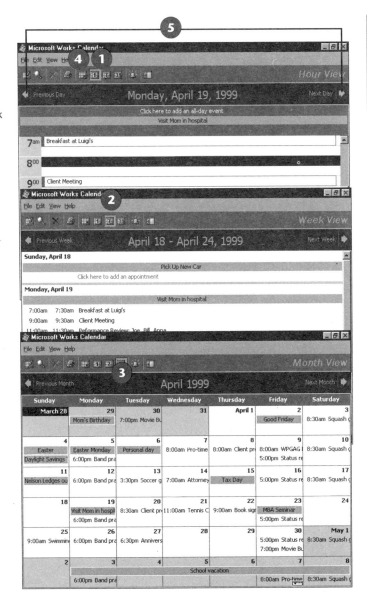

Entering a New Appointment

An *appointment* is any meeting or engagement at a specific time. It's a good idea to enter a new appointment into Works Calendar as soon as you make it, so you won't forget to do so. If you're in a hurry, you can just click a date on the calendar and type some information to enter a new appointment. However, it takes only a few seconds longer to make a complete entry, with reminders set to alert you anywhere from a week to 15 minutes before the appointment.

TIP

Scheduling almost-recurrent events. *If you have an event or appointment that isn't strictly recurring, for example, if there is a meeting on the first three Thursdays of each month, enter it as a regular recurring event, and then delete the exceptions by right-clicking them and choosing Delete Item from the shortcut menu that appears.*

Enter an Appointment

1. Click the New Appointment button on the toolbar.

2. Type a title and a location for the appointment.

3. Click the Category button and click the check box to choose a category, and then click OK.

4. If the All-Day Event check box is selected, click to clear it.

5. Choose the time and day when the appointment begins and ends.

6. Type notes or comments.

7. Choose a reminder.

8. To repeat an appointment, click the Make This Appointment Repeat check box and click the Recurrence button.

9. Select the recurring options you want.

10. Click the OK button in the Recurrence Options dialog box.

11. Click the OK button in the New Appointment dialog box.

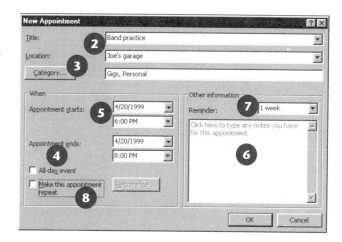

Choose daily, weekly, monthly, or yearly intervals.

Refine the periods for the appointments, such as every day or every weekday.

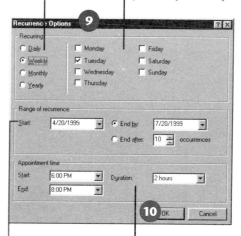

Specify the length of time the appointment should be repeated.

Confirm or modify the start and end times, as well as the duration of the appointment.

Entering Events

An *event* is an activity that doesn't occur at a specific time of day, such as an anniversary, vacation, or educational seminar. Anything that takes place at an unfixed time during a day, or which spans more than one day, can be entered into Works Calendar as an event.

TIP

Change an appointment into an event. *Right-click the appointment you want to convert to an event, and choose Open from the shortcut menu that appears. Click the All-Day Event check box and click the OK button to apply the change.*

Enter an Event

1 In the Week or Month view, right-click the day the event begins, and choose New All-Day Event from the shortcut menu.

2 Type a title and location for the event.

3 Click the Category button and click the check box next to the event's category.

4 Click OK.

5 Choose the day when the event begins and ends.

6 Type any notes to yourself, such as driving directions or comments.

7 To repeat an event, click the Make This Appointment Repeat check box and click the Recurrence button.

8 Select the recurring options you want.

9 Choose a reminder.

10 Click the OK button in the Recurrence Options dialog box, if necessary, and then click the OK button in the New Appointment dialog box to return to the calendar.

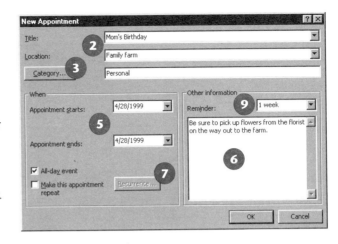

Choose daily, weekly, monthly, or yearly intervals.

Refine the periods for the appointments, such as every day or every weekday.

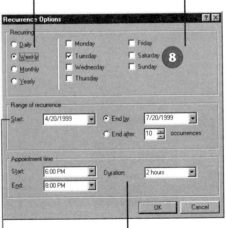

Specify the length of time the appointment should be repeated.

Confirm or modify the start and end times, as well as the duration of the appointment.

Categorizing Appointments

Although assigning each event or appointment to a category is optional, doing so is a great way to help you organize your time. Calendar can classify appointments using built-in classifications, or using categories you define. You can select more than one category for a single appointment, and change the categories for existing appointments.

TIP

Create new categories.
Create categories that help you organize your appointments. Instead of classifying everything work-related under Business, define categories like Client Meetings, Presentations, or Trips. Because you can assign several categories to each appointment, engagements can be listed under one general classification and as many sub-classifications as apply.

Create or Modify a Category

1. Right-click any event on the calendar and choose Categories from the short-cut menu that appears.

2. Click the Edit Categories button.

3. To modify an existing category, select it and click the Delete or Rename button.

4. To create a new category, type the name and click the Add button.

5. Click OK to apply your edits.

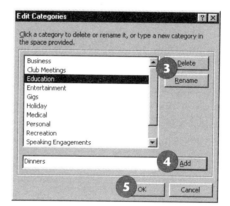

7

Print by categories. *Works Calendar uses a special dialog box for printing. If you show or hide categories, you can ask Works to print appointments that are displayed, either by day or monthly listings.*

Organize client appointments. *If you have several different clients, define a category for each. You can easily search for all upcoming engagements with a particular client.*

Find appointments in deleted categories. *If you delete a category, you may find that appointments formerly in that category don't appear in your schedule. Click the Show Category Filter button, if necessary, to view the Category Filter list, and make sure the Not Categorized check box is selected.*

Change an Event or Appointment's Category

1. Right-click an existing event and choose Open from the menu that appears.

2. Click the Category button and click the check box next to the category you want in the Choose Categories dialog box.

3. Click OK to apply the category to the event or appointment.

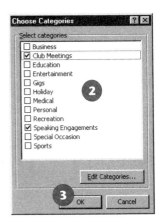

Viewing Appointments by Categories

You can elect to show or hide appointments in day, week, or month view based on the categories, such as Business or Personal, that you've applied to the appointments. You can have Works Calendar show you a list of all your business appointments so you can add them to a to do list. Or you might want to see all your upcoming special occasions to plan gift buying.

SEE ALSO

For information creating and applying categories, see "Categorizing Appointments" on page 120.

Show or Hide Categories

1. Click the Show Category Filter button on the toolbar, if necessary, to reveal the Appointment Categories list.

2. Click to select or clear the check boxes next to the categories you want to view or hide.

3. Click Show Appointments In All Categories in the Category Filter drop-down list to display all appointments.

4. Click Show Only Uncategorized Appointments in the Category Filter drop-down list to see uncategorized appointments.

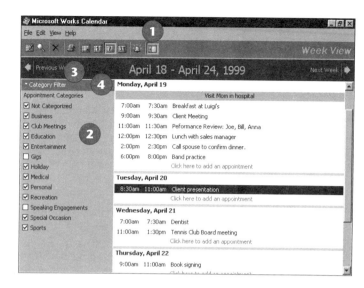

Setting Reminders

Works Calendar can warn you ahead of time with a handy pop-up reminder when an appointment or event is scheduled to take place. The prompting can be set to take place anywhere from 15 minutes to a full week before the event. The reminder appears on your screen immediately if you are using Works Calendar when the reminder time occurs (or the first time you use the tool after the time has passed).

TIP

View or edit all active reminders. *Click the Reminders button on the toolbar to create a list of active reminders. You can open and edit any of them, or cancel any or all of them.*

Set or Remove a Reminder

1 Create a new appointment by clicking the New Appointment button on the toolbar, or open an existing appointment by double-clicking the appointment on the calendar.

2 If an existing appointment is a recurring event, Works Calendar will ask whether you want to edit only this event, or all the events in that series.

◆ Click Open This Occurrence if you want to add the reminder only to this instance of the event.

◆ Click Open The Series if you want to add the reminder to all instances of the event.

3 Click OK if you choose either of these.

4 Choose when you want the reminder to appear. To remove a reminder, choose None.

5 Click OK to apply the reminder setting.

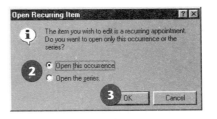

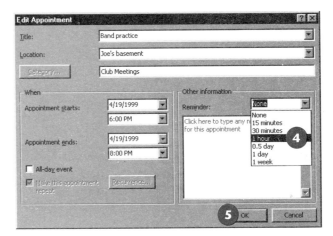

Modifying an Appointment

You'll frequently have to change an existing appointment to a new day, time, or location. You may have to cancel the appointment or event entirely. Works Calendar allows you to make these changes quickly. You can even modify one instance of a recurring event without changing the others in the series.

Change an Appointment

1. Right-click the appointment or event you want to change on the calendar, and choose Open from the shortcut menu that appears.

2. If the appointment you want to edit is a recurring event, Works Calendar will ask whether you want to edit only this event, or all occurrences of the event.

   ◆ Click Open This Occurrence if you want to edit only this instance of the event.

   ◆ Click Open The Series if you want to edit all instances of the event.

   ◆ Click OK if you choose either of these.

3. Make all the changes you want to the appointment or event in the Edit Appointment dialog box.

4. Click OK to apply your changes.

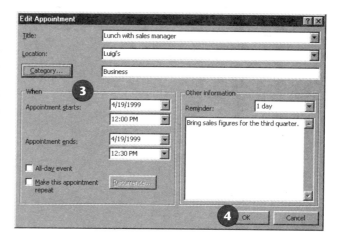

Delete an Appointment

1. Click the appointment you want to delete in your calendar.

2. Click the Delete button on the toolbar.

3. If the appointment you are deleting is a recurring event, Works Calendar will ask whether you want to delete only this event, or all occurrences of the event.

4. Click OK to delete the appointment if it is a recurring event.

5. Click Yes in the Confirm Deletion dialog box that appears.

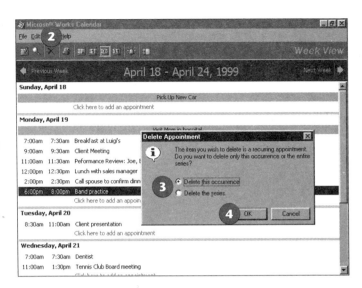

Searching Your Calendar

One of the best features of a computerized calendar is the ability to search through it quickly for specific appointments. Can't remember when your next dentist appointment is—or even if you've remembered to schedule one? Works Calendar can search your entries and find the appointments you're looking for in a second or two. You can search by keywords, time, or categories.

TIP

Sort a list of appointments.
When Calendar produces a list of appointments it finds after a search, you can click the Subject, Start, End, or Category headers in the list to sort the list.

Search for an Event or Appointment

1. Click the Find button on the toolbar.

2. Choose the tab containing the criteria you want to search with and select the options you want.

3. Click the Find Now button.

4. When the list of appointments appears, scroll through the appointments and click either the Open Item button (to view the appointment) or the Delete Item button (to remove it).

5. If Works Calendar is unable to locate the appointment you are looking for, click the New Search button and enter new search criteria.

Click the Keyword tab to search for appointments based on one or more words you type.

Click the Time tab to specify a rough starting and ending time span to search.

Click the Category tab to look only for appointments within certain categories.

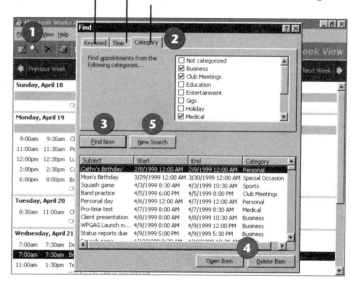

Sharing Calendar Information

You can share your Works Calendar information with others. An appointment can be exported as an HTML document that can be viewed with Microsoft Internet Explorer or another Web browser; as a tab-delimited format file that can be imported by calendar programs that support that format; or in the VCalendar format used by some other calendar applications. Works Calendar can also send appointment information to a friend or colleague in an e-mail message.

TIP

Import by compatible programs. *Works Calendar's appointment information can be imported by compatible programs such as Microsoft Outlook.*

Share Calendar

1. Select an appointment, and choose Send To E-Mail from the File menu to e-mail your information.

2. From the File menu, point to Export and choose VCalendar, HTML, or Tab-Delimited.

3. Choose whether to format the appointments in day, week, or month views and choose starting and ending dates.

4. In the Include area, choose whether to send only appointments currently selected in the Category Filter view or to send all appointments.

5. Click OK.

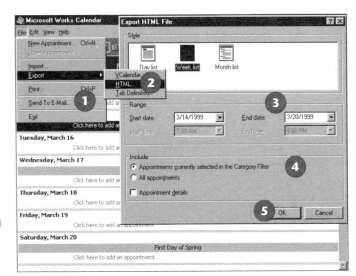

Printing with Works Applications

As ubiquitous as computers have become, the ability to print out paper copies of what you see on your display screen is one of the most valuable and widely used capabilities of applications like Microsoft Works. Printed letters can be mailed anywhere in the world—even to people who don't have e-mail. You can drop a copy of a paper report in a briefcase and review it at your leisure without having to remember to bring your laptop along. School reports, greeting cards, notes for speeches, newsletters, résumés, and countless other documents can be printed attractively using Works.

Printing good-looking documents is an especially easy skill to master because Works' tools all use the same procedures for printing, and these, in turn, closely resemble the methods used to print in other Microsoft Windows applications. You can quickly learn how to format pages, set margins, choose paper size and orientation, and add page numbers, headers, or footers. Then you can apply what you've learned to every document you print, whether it's a spreadsheet, word processing document, or database report.

Selecting a Printer

Some of the settings for printing pages change when you switch from one printer to another, so you should select the printer you are going to use to print a document before you do anything else. If you have only one printer connected to your computer, Works selects it for you automatically. If you have several printers that you use with your computer, or are connected to a network with more than one printer available, you should change your printer selection each time you want to use a different device.

TIP
Choose a default printer.
If you have more than one printer available, you can specify which one is used by default. Choose Settings from the Start menu, and then choose Printers. Right-click the printer you want to use and select Set As Default from the shortcut menu that appears.

Select a Printer

1 Choose Print from the File menu.

2 Choose a printer from the Name drop-down list.

3 Click OK.

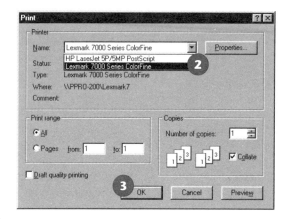

Setting Margins

Margins are the blank areas around the edges of your page at the top, bottom, and sides. Margins provide a frame for your document and also serve to improve the appearance and readability of the text. For example, wide margins make the lines of text shorter and easier to read. Narrow margins let you pack more text onto a page. Works allows you to set margins on all four sides of the page, and to set the distance between any header or footer you have included and the rest of the text.

Set Margins

1. Choose Page Setup from the File menu.

2. Click the Margins tab, if necessary.

3. Enter margin values in the Margins area.

   ◆ Click the up and down arrows to change the width of the top, bottom, left, and right margins.

   ◆ Type a value directly into the box for each margin, using " (quotation marks) to indicate inches, or cm, mm, pi, or pt to specify margins in centimeters, millimeters, picas, or points, respectively.

4. In the From Edge area, click the up and down arrows to adjust the distance between the header or footer from the rest of the text on each page, or type a value directly into the box for each margin.

5. Click OK to apply the margin settings.

Preview of page margin settings.

Click to reset margins to default values.

8

Choosing Paper Source, Orientation, and Size

While most of the documents you print will probably be on standard-sized paper, you'll sometimes want to use special paper or envelopes. More frequently, you'll need to change from portrait (vertical) orientation to landscape (horizontal) orientation to print, say, a wide spreadsheet on a single piece of paper. If your printer is equipped with multiple paper drawers or requires special papers or envelopes to be fed through a specific tray, you can specify that as well.

Choose Paper Source and Orientation

1. Choose Page Setup from the File menu.

2. Click the Source, Size & Orientation tab, if necessary.

3. Click either Portrait (for vertical orientation) or Landscape (for horizontal orientation).

4. From the choices available for your particular printer, choose the tray or paper cassette you want to use, such as Default Tray, Manual Feed, Envelope Feed, Automatic Feeder, or some other option.

5. Click OK.

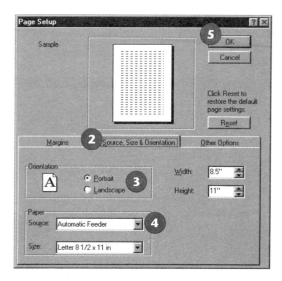

Choose Paper Size

1. Choose Page Setup from the File menu.

2. Click the Source, Size & Orientation tab, if necessary.

3. Choose a paper size from the Size drop-down list.

   ◆ If you are using a standard paper size, such as Letter, Legal, A4, or #10 envelope, select the size from the list.

   ◆ If you want to specify another paper size, select Custom Size from the list and click the Width and Height arrows to specify the measurements of your paper.

   ◆ Custom sizes can also be typed directly into the Width and Height boxes. Use " (quotation marks) to enter sizes in inches, or cm, mm, pi, or pt to specify margins in centimeters, millimeters, picas, or points, respectively.

4. Click OK to apply the settings.

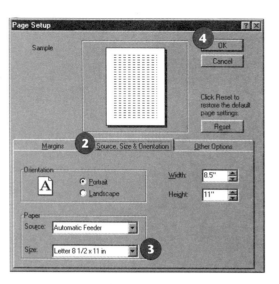

8

Setting Page Numbers, Headers, and Footers

You can choose which number will be used as the starting page number printed on a document (the default is 1). For example, if you were printing a book or similar document a chapter at a time, you would want the numbering for a new chapter to begin with the number after last one in the previous chapter. In addition, you might not want any number to print on the first page of a document such as a letter. You can also choose whether a header or footer is printed on the first page of a document.

TIP

Print gridlines and headers. *If you're printing a spreadsheet or database, the Options tab includes check boxes for showing or hiding gridlines or headers for rows and columns or fields.*

Set Page Numbers, Headers, and Footers

1 Choose Page Setup from the File menu.

2 Click the Other Options tab, if necessary.

3 In the Starting Page Number box, type the number to be used for the first page of the document, or click the up or down arrow to choose a value.

4 Click the No Header On First Page or No Footer On First Page check box to turn headers or footers on or off for the first page.

5 If your document includes footnotes, you can have them printed either at the end of your document or at the bottom of the page by selecting or clearing the Print Footnotes At End check box.

6 Click OK to apply the settings.

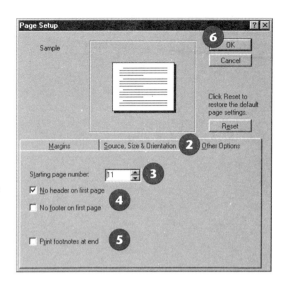

Previewing Pages before Printing

You'll frequently want to preview a page before printing it to make sure it looks the way you intended. Previewing is a good way to spot margins that are too wide or too narrow, paragraph alignment that doesn't look right, or just gather an over-view of how your pages will look. In Print Preview mode, you can move quickly from page to page and zoom in and out to examine pages in as much detail as you want.

TIP
Display charts as printed.
Although Works displays spreadsheet charts in color, it may convert the colors to patterns when printing on a black-and-white printer. To see how your chart will look when printed, choose Display As Printed from the View menu.

Preview a Page

1. Place the insertion point at the beginning of the document or to the page where you want to begin your preview.

2. Click the Print Preview button on the toolbar.

   ◆ Click the Previous or Next button to move to different pages.

   ◆ Click the Zoom In or Zoom Out button to expand or narrow your view of the current page.

   ◆ Click the Cancel button to return to your document to make changes or if you've decided not to print the document.

   ◆ Click the Print button to print the document.

Enlarge view of chart.

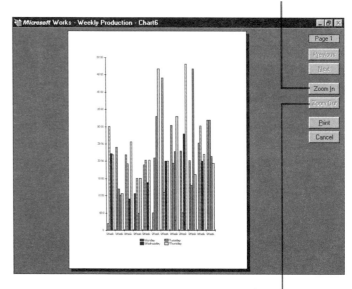

Reduce view of chart.

8

Printing

Once you've made all your settings and previewed your document, you're ready to print it. You can specify several printing options, including which pages should be printed, the number of copies, and whether you want the copies collated. When printing starts, you can change the sequence of print jobs if you decide you'd like a particular set of pages to be printed first.

Select Pages to Print and Number of Copies

1. Choose Print from the File menu.

2. Choose the pages to be printed in the Print Range area.

   ◆ Click All if you want to print all the pages in the document.

   ◆ Click Pages and type the beginning and ending pages to print only selected pages in a document.

3. Type the number of copies you want in the Number Of Copies box, or click the arrows to specify a value.

4. Click the Collate check box if you want the copies collated.

5. Click OK to print the document.

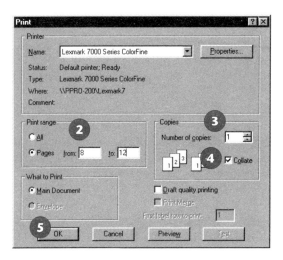

Choose chart printing options. *If you're printing a chart, you can select only the number of copies to print. There are no page numbers to select.*

Cancel a print job. *To delete a print job before it starts to print, point to Settings on the Start menu and choose Printers. Double-click the printer that is printing your jobs. Click the name of a document not being printed, and choose Cancel from the Document menu.*

Set Sequence of Jobs Being Printed

1 Point to Settings on the Start menu.

2 Choose Printers.

3 Double-click the printer that is currently printing your jobs.

4 Click the name of any document not already being printed that you want to move, and drag it to its new position in the print order.

Document is being printed.

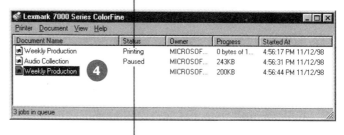

This document hasn't been started yet.

Browsing the Web with Internet Explorer

Microsoft Internet Explorer 4 is a versatile tool you can use to explore the Internet, access computers on a network at work, or even browse your own desktop. With Internet Explorer installed on your computer you can jump directly to your favorite Web sites, receive specialized content from online channels, and explore the files and folders on your own computer using the same navigational skills. Internet Explorer can also be your gateway to information for personal or business research through search engines that locate and access Web pages containing a rich treasure-trove of information. Internet Explorer can also lead you to great files available online, such as free clip art for newsletters, trial software packages, and entertaining multimedia clips.

Viewing the Internet Explorer Window

Title bar
Name of the Web page you're viewing

Links bar
Buttons to link to several Microsoft Web sites and some of your own favorites

Standard toolbar
Buttons to access and move around Web pages and work in Internet Explorer

Menu bar
Commands for moving around the Web

Address bar
Address of current document or Web page. You can type in an address you want to jump to.

Explorer bar
The Favorites list, History list, channels, and results of searches

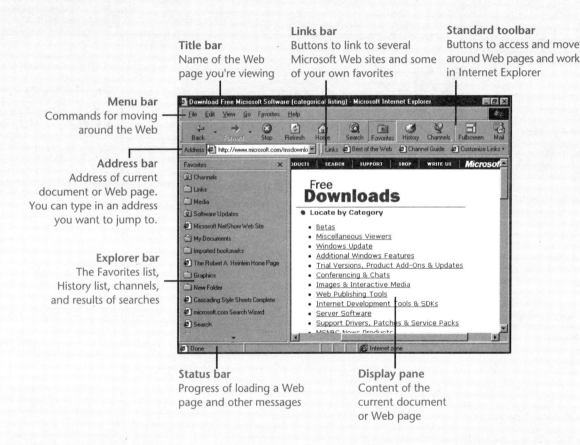

Status bar
Progress of loading a Web page and other messages

Display pane
Content of the current document or Web page

Getting Started with Internet Explorer

If Internet Explorer is your default Web browser, it will start automatically whenever you click a Web link on your desktop or in another program (such as in an e-mail message). You can also start Internet Explorer from the Start menu.

TIP

Set Internet Explorer as your default Web browser.
You can set Internet Explorer as the browser that Windows loads automatically when you click a Web link. Choose Internet Options from the View menu, click the Programs tab, and click the Internet Explorer Should Check To See If It Is The Default Browser check box.

Start Internet Explorer

1 Click the Start button.

2 Point to Programs.

3 Point to Internet Explorer.

4 Click Internet Explorer.

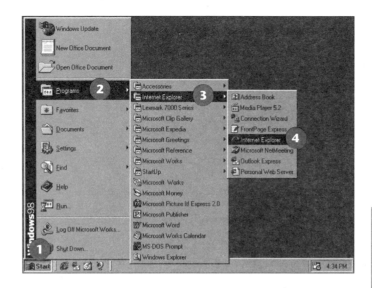

Connecting to the Internet

Internet Explorer can connect you to the Internet once you provide it with some information about your Internet account and your *Internet service provider* (ISP). For most accounts, all you'll need to know is the phone number of the ISP, the name you use to *log on* (connect) to the service provider, and your password. If you'll be using Internet Explorer or Microsoft Outlook Express to send e-mail or to retrieve or post articles to newsgroups, you'll also need to know the name of the computer(s) your ISP uses for those services. Some ISPs require extra information to log on; you can ask the ISP system administrator for step-by-step instructions for your particular service. Once you've set up a dial-up connection, Internet Explorer will use it to connect to the Internet.

Create a Dial-up Connection

1. Click the Start button, point to Programs, point to Internet Explorer, and then click Connection Wizard.

2. Click the option button for the setup you want to use.

3. Click Next to continue.

4. Read the information in each wizard dialog box, and then enter the required information. Click Next to continue.

5. In the final wizard dialog box, click Finish to create the dial-up connection Internet Explorer will use by default.

Click if you want the Internet Connection Wizard to help you choose a new Internet service provider and sign up for an account.

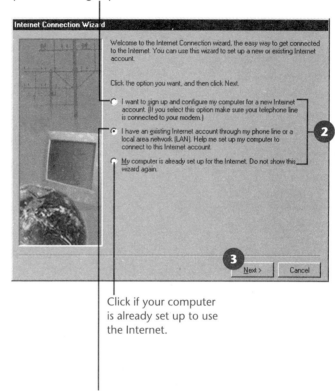

Click if your computer is already set up to use the Internet.

Click if you already have an Internet service provider or you connect to the Internet through a local area network and want to set up your computer to use your existing Internet account.

Browsing the Web

To browse Web sites, all you need to do is type the Web address in the Address bar, or choose a page you've already visited by clicking one of the addresses shown when you click the drop-down arrow on the Address bar, or click a *link*. A link is a graphic or text connection that tells your browser to jump to a different part of the page, a different page, or a page on another Web site.

SEE ALSO

For information on saving favorite pages for later visits, see "Creating a Favorites List" on page 150.

Enter Web Addresses

1. In the Address bar, type the Web page address and press the Enter key. Click a link in the Display pane.

2. Choose Open from the File menu and type a Web page address in the Open dialog box.

Choose an address from the drop-down list here.

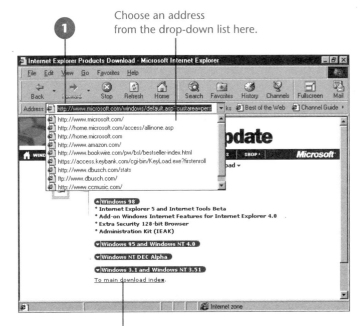

Click a link anywhere in the browser window.

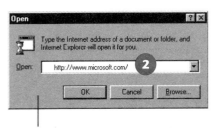

Use the Open command on the File menu to enter a Web address.

Navigating the Web

Internet Explorer tracks your visits to the Web, making it easy to retrace your steps to revisit a site you've already examined, or to jump ahead from that earlier site to one you visited later in your travels. For example, you might want to go back to an earlier Web page to check a fact, then move to a more recent page to continue your research.

Internet Explorer can also complete many Web addresses for you by using its AutoComplete feature. If you type a partial address in the Address bar, Internet Explorer will search from among the pages you've visited recently for a match. You can accept the match by pressing the Enter key, or continue typing the full address before pressing the Enter key.

Move Backward or Forward

1. To move forward or backward one Web page at a time, click the Forward or Back button on the Standard toolbar.

2. To move forward or backward to a specific Web page, click the Back or Forward button drop-down arrow and select the Web page you want to visit.

3. Click the drop-down arrow in the Address bar and choose a Web page address from the list of places you've previously visited.

4. Begin to type a Web address you have recently visited, and let Internet Explorer's AutoComplete feature fill in as much of the rest of the address as it can. Click the Enter key to accept the suggestion.

Move backward. Move forward.

Type partial address and let AutoComplete fill in the rest.

Choose previously visited Web page.

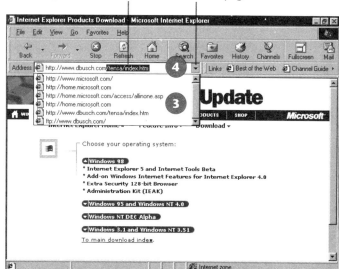

Stop a page from loading or refresh a page. *If you find you no longer want to view a page that is loading, you can stop it by clicking the Stop button on the Standard toolbar. To reload a page (to refresh the information on page, or to restart a canceled download of the page), click the Refresh button on the Standard toolbar.*

Return quickly to your home page. *Choose a default home page for Internet Explorer to display by choosing Internet Options from the View menu. Type the page's address in the Address box on the General tab. You can return quickly to that page by clicking the Home button on the Standard toolbar.*

Working with Web Buttons

 Click a toolbar button to perform an action, open a menu with more options, or open a dialog box.

WEB BUTTONS		
To do this	**Click the**	
Stop a page from loading	Stop button	⊗ Stop
Reload the current page	Refresh button	Refresh
Jump to your home page	Home button	Home
Find a Web page	Search button	Search
Add or find a favorite location	Favorites button	Favorites
View a list of previously visited pages	History button	History
View available channels	Channels button	Channels
View a Web page in full frame view	Full Screen button	Fullscreen
Send an e-mail message	Mail button	Mail

9

Viewing Web Sites with a History List

The History folder automatically tracks all the Web sites you visit over the course of days or weeks. You can return to any of these Web pages quickly by choosing sites you want to revisit from folders shown in the History list in the Explorer bar. You can delete sites from your History list, or clear the entire list to start over or save some hard disk space.

View a Web Site from the History List

1. Click the History button on the Standard toolbar.

2. Click a week or day to view or hide the folders with the list of sites visited then.

3. Click the folder for the Web site you want to view to see all the pages you visited at that site.

4. Click a page within the Web site to return to that page.

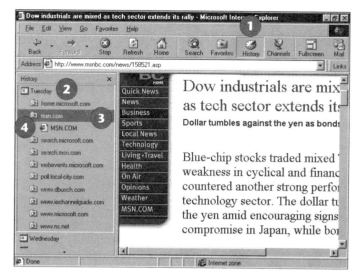

TIP

Hide the History list. *To hide close the History list in the Explorer bar so you can view the full Display pane, click the History button again on the toolbar.*

TIP

Remove a page from the History list. *To remove an item from your History list, right-click the page and choose Delete from the shortcut menu that appears.*

SEE ALSO

For information on adding a page in your History list to your Favorites list, see "Creating a Favorites List" on page 150.

Clear or Size Your History Folder

1. Choose Internet Options from the View menu.

2. Click the General tab.

3. Click the Clear History button to remove all the pages from your History folder.

4. Enter the number of days you want to keep links in the History folder before they are deleted automatically.

5. Click Apply to apply the changes.

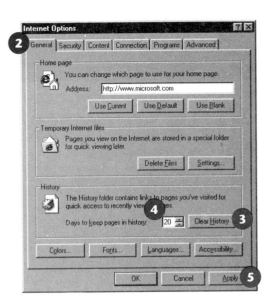

9

Searching for Information on the Web

There's a wealth of information available on the Web—if you know how to find it. There are Web sites called *search engines* that index many different pages and provide a quick way of searching for the information you need. You'll also find *all-in-one* search pages that offer gateways to several different search engines from one convenient site. Each search engine might use slightly different terminology, such as using a button labeled *Search, Find, Go,* or *Seek* to launch a search, but most are easy to use.

Search with the Search Button

1 Click the Search button on the Standard toolbar.

2 Click the Choose A Search Engine drop-down arrow, and then select the search provider you want to use.

3 Type the keyword you want to use for the search in the box provided by the search engine, and then click the Search, Find, Go, or Seek button provided by the search provider.

4 Click the result you want to view.

5 When you are finished, click the Close button or click the Search button on the Standard toolbar.

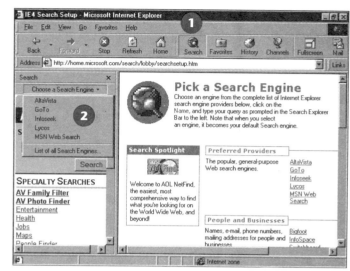

Be specific in your search. *Type keywords that will narrow your search. For example, type "Chicago blues harmonica" rather than "Blues" or "Music" to locate information about blues harmonica players.*

Use quotation marks to pair words. *Most search engines will look for words individually unless you put a group of them inside quotation marks. For example, entering **nature photography** will return lists of pages about nature, or photography, but if you use "nature photography" instead, the search engine will look specifically for entries in that category.*

Do a follow-up search. *If you don't find what you are looking for the first time, try different keywords, do an advanced search, or try a different search engine. Odds are the information you are looking for is on the Web: you just need to ask the right questions to find it.*

Perform an Advanced Search

1. Click the Search button on the Standard toolbar.

2. Click the Choose A Search Engine drop-down arrow, and then select the search provider you want to use.

3. Click your provider's advanced search button.

4. Type the keyword(s) you want to use for the search.

5. Choose other options available from the provider for an advanced search.

6. Click the Search, Find, Go, or Seek button provided by the search provider.

7. Click the result you want to view.

8. When you are finished, click the Close button or click the Search button on the Standard toolbar.

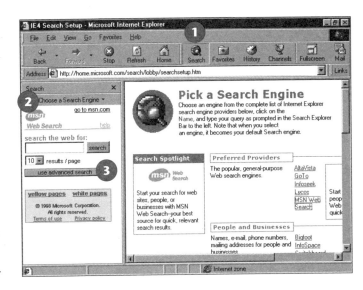

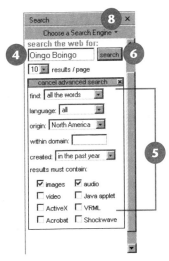

Creating a Favorites List

If you often visit certain Web sites, you can add them to your Favorites list. Then you'll be able to jump directly to those sites by choosing the page you want from your Favorites list. You can access your favorite pages from the Favorites menu, or by clicking the Favorites button in the Standard toolbar to open the Favorites list in the Explorer bar.

Create a Favorites List

1. Open the Web site you want to add to your Favorites list.

2. Right-click on the page or any link on the page in the Display pane, and choose Add To Favorites.

3. Type the name you want to use for the Favorite.

4. Click Create In to add the site to a specific folder.

5. Click OK to add the site to your Favorites folder.

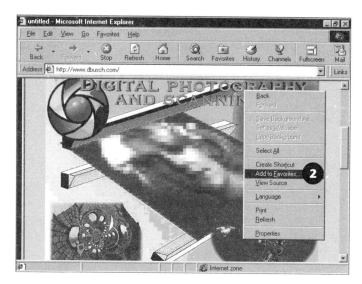

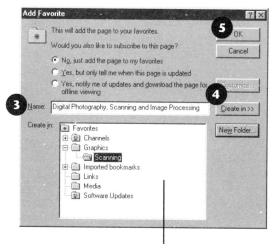

Shows folders in which Favorites can be placed.

TIP

Drag a page to your Favorites list. *You can drag a page (by dragging its icon from the Address bar) or a link to the Favorites button on the Standard toolbar to place that item in your Favorites list.*

TIP

Hide the Favorites list. *To hide the Favorites list, click the Favorites button on the Standard toolbar.*

TIP

Drag from the Address bar. *You can place the current page in your Favorites list by dragging its icon in the Address bar to the Favorites button.*

SEE ALSO

For information on subscribing to pages in your Favorites list, see "Subscribing to Web Sites and Channels" on page 156.

View Your Favorites

1. Click the Favorites button on the Standard toolbar.

2. Click a folder in the Favorites list to open or close the list of sites visited.

3. Click a page within one of the folders to jump to that Favorite.

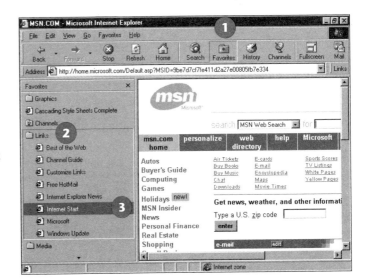

Maintaining Your Favorites List

You can update your Favorites list to purge old pages you no longer want. It's also easy to reorganize your favorite pages into easy-to-access folders, with names like *Research* or *Spanish Cities* to categorize the kind of information they contain. You'll want to maintain your Favorites list regularly to make it most useful to you.

Organize a Favorites List

1 Choose Organize Favorites from the Favorites menu.

2 Click a folder to view the folders and pages within that folder.

3 Click the folder or file you want to move, rename, or delete.

4 Apply the change you want to make.

- ◆ Click Move to move the site to another folder within the Favorites folder.

- ◆ Click Rename to rename the site.

- ◆ Click Delete to remove the site from your list of favorites.

5 Click the New Folder button to create a new folder.

6 Click the Close button when you are finished.

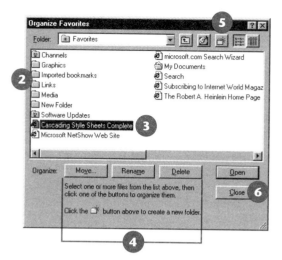

Add favorite pages from the History list. *You can drag any pages from your History list to the Favorites button on the Standard toolbar to add them to your Favorites list.*

Add favorite pages to the Links bar. *You might want frequently used pages to appear on the Links bar. Click within the pages and drag them to the Links folder in your Favorites list to add them automatically.*

Open a favorite page from the Start menu. *Open the Start menu, point to Favorites, and choose the page you want to visit from the Favorites list.*

Delete a Favorite

1. Click the Favorites button on the Standard toolbar.

2. Right-click the page or folder you want to delete in the Favorites list.

3. Choose Delete from the menu that appears.

Saving Text and Files from a Web Page

Web sites often provide free trial programs, documents, images, multimedia clips, and other files you can download to your computer. However, Internet Explorer allows you to download other items, including most images, buttons, and other graphics you see on a page, plus the *HTML* (Hypertext Markup Language—the programming-like code used to format Web pages) pages and their backgrounds themselves. In addition, you can copy text that appears on your screen and paste it into other applications. When downloading or copying anything from the Web, you should be aware of legal restrictions that can apply to reuse of material found on the Internet.

Download a File

1 Visit the Web page that has the file you want to download.

2 Right-click the link to the file you want to save, and click Save Target As on the shortcut menu.

◆ Right-click an image and choose either Save Picture As or Set As Wallpaper to save the image on your hard disk.

◆ Right-click the background of a page and choose Save Background As to download the background image.

◆ Right-click the background of a page and choose View Source to open the HTML source code in Notepad. Choose Save from Notepad's File menu to store the HTML page on your hard disk drive.

◆ Right-click links to multimedia clips or program files and choose Save Link As from the shortcut menu.

3 Choose the folder in which you want to save the file.

4 Click the Save button.

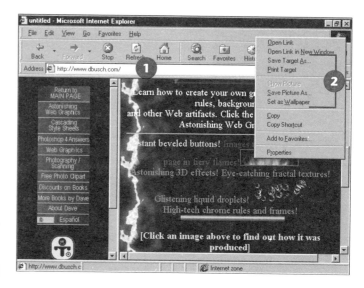

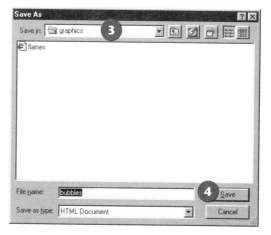

Save an HTML page to your hard disk drive. *You can also download the HTML code for the Web page you are viewing by choosing Save As from Internet Explorer's File menu. Only the page's text, not its pictures, are saved.*

Find out how much space a graphic requires. *Right-click the image, and then click Properties on the shortcut menu to view the size of a graphic before you download it.*

Copy a graphic directly. *Right-click the graphic you want to copy and choose Copy from the shortcut menu. Switch to an open document in the application where you want to copy the image, and choose Paste from the Edit menu. Internet Explorer will download the image directly into the document.*

Copy and Paste Text

1. Visit the Web page with the text you want to copy.

2. Drag with the mouse to select the text.

   ◆ To select all the text on a page, choose Select All from the Edit menu.

3. Choose Copy from the Edit menu.

4. Switch to the application where you want to paste the text.

5. Place the insertion point where you want to insert the text.

6. Choose Paste from the Edit menu.

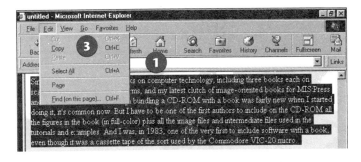

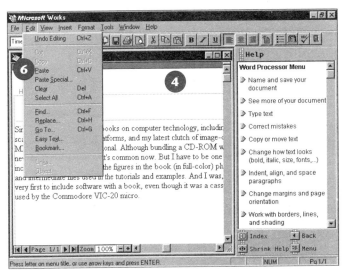

Subscribing to Web Sites and Channels

Many Web sites resemble newspapers or magazines: they offer frequent updates, sometimes daily, of information you might want to keep abreast of, including weather, sports scores, or news. Internet Explorer allows you to *subscribe* to pages, and receive the revised content at intervals you specify. Because updating subscribed pages is handled by Internet Explorer, you can subscribe to any page you like.

Other Web sites provide *channels* of information that can be delivered to your desktop. Channels are pages of information prepared and regularly updated by an information provider for delivery to those who have requested them. You must subscribe to a channel to receive it.

Subscribe to a Web Site

1 Open the Web site you want to subscribe to.

2 Choose Add To Favorites from the Favorites menu.

3 Type a name for your Web page, and then click OK if you don't want to customize your subscription further.

4 If you want to customize a subscription, click the Customize button.

5 Click the Yes option to be notified in an e-mail message that a page has changed.

6 Click Next to continue.

7 Enter a user name and password if the site requires it.

8 Click Finish

9 Click OK.

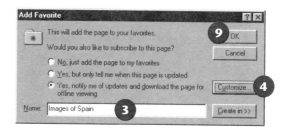

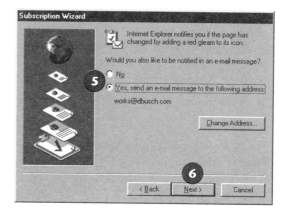

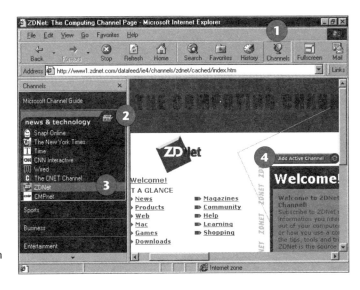

TIP

Subscribe to a channel quickly. *If you already know you want to subscribe to a channel without previewing it first, right-click the channel name in the Channels bar and follow the instructions in the wizard that starts.*

TIP

Delete a channel from the Channel bar. *Right-click the channel you want to delete, and choose Delete from the shortcut menu.*

TIP

Update your subscriptions immediately. *You don't have to wait for the update interval you've specified to pass. Choose Update All Subscriptions from the Favorites menu.*

Subscribe to a Channel

1. Click the Channels button on the Standard toolbar.

2. Click a channel category.

3. Choose the channel you want to subscribe to.

4. Click the Add Active Channels button found on the Web site.

5. Click the subscription option you want.

6. Click the Customize button to specify options such as whether you want to be notified of a channel update by e-mail.

7. Click OK.

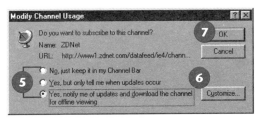

Viewing Channels

The Channel bar is your gateway to viewing all the channels you have subscribed to, as well as the "table of contents" you'll use to choose which channels you want to add to your list. To view a channel, just click a channel category and then click the channel you want to see.

SEE ALSO

See "Subscribe to a Channel" on page 157 for information on adding a subscription to a channel.

View a Channel

1. Click the Channels button on the Standard toolbar.

2. Click a channel to view the channel or click a category to expand that category.

3. If the channel offers multiple Web pages from which to choose, click the channel to display the list of other pages, and then click the page you want to view.

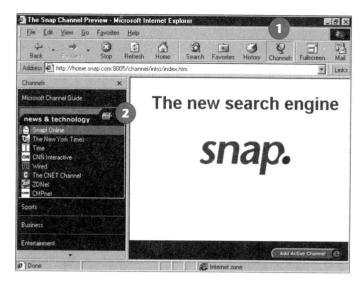

Managing Subscriptions

From time to time, you'll need to unsubscribe to Web pages or channels that become defunct, or which no longer pique your interest. You may also have to update your subscription information when a site requires a username and password but didn't ask for them before. You may also want to change how your subscription is updated.

Manage Subscriptions

1. Choose Manage Subscriptions from the Favorites menu.

2. Right-click the Web site or channel for the subscription you want to modify and then click Properties.

3. Click the Subscription tab to subscribe or unsubscribe or review subscription summaries.

4. Click the Receiving tab to set subscription notification by e-mail and download options.

5. Click the Schedule tab to specify when you want to update a subscription.

6. Click OK.

7. Click the File menu and then click the Close button.

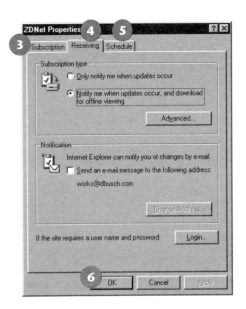

9

Exchanging E-Mail Messages with Outlook Express

Microsoft Outlook Express provides an easy way to send or receive e-mail. You can send messages to individuals, provide courtesy copies or blind copies to others, or send e-mail to distribution groups you define. Once you receive messages, you can use Outlook Express to sort and organize them into folders so you can retrieve them quickly.

This program also can track appointments, store contact information such as names and addresses, keep a journal, and maintain a computerized to-do list.

It won't take long for you to learn to use Outlook Express, because it organizes e-mail and other entries the same way Microsoft Windows does: with folders that you can name, move, place inside other folders, and arrange exactly as you might with physical folders in a file cabinet.

You'll find that exchanging e-mail with friends and colleagues is a great way to keep in touch, conduct business, and share information over the Internet.

Viewing the Outlook Express Window

Compose mail.

View items in selected folders.

Address Book

Name of folder that is currently open

Navigate folders.

Choose folders to view.

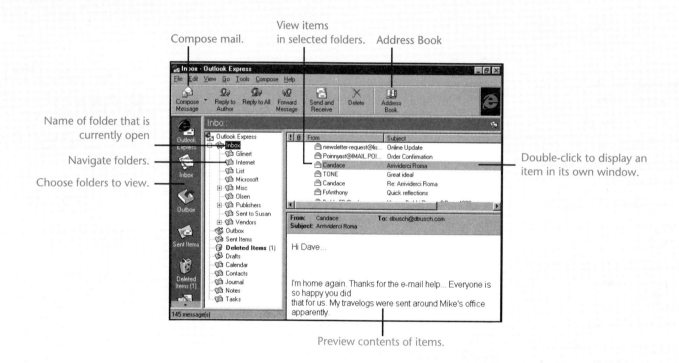

Double-click to display an item in its own window.

Preview contents of items.

Receiving E-Mail Messages

Once you've set up Outlook Express with information about your e-mail account, you can receive e-mail with a single click. Using Outlook Express, you can log on to your e-mail provider, download messages automatically, and deposit the messages in a folder for sorting and organizing. You don't have to open an e-mail message to see what's inside. Outlook Express provides a handy preview pane you can use to peek inside your messages as you browse through the stack of incoming mail. In the following procedures, I'll assume you've already logged on to your network or ISP correctly.

TIP

Locate new messages.
Messages you haven't read appear in boldface type.

Receive E-Mail Messages

1. Click the Send And Receive button on the toolbar.

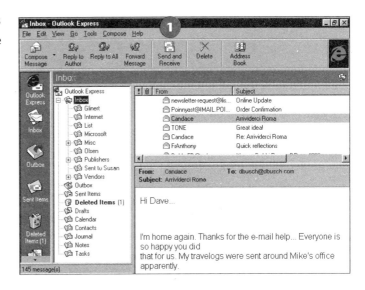

Outlook connects to your e-mail provider.

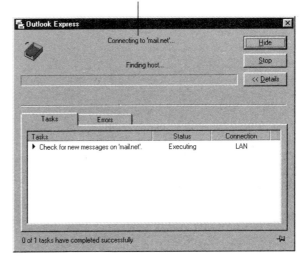

Viewing Messages and Attachments

You won't need much practice to become adept at viewing messages with Outlook Express' intuitive folder organization. Even if you receive a large number of e-mail messages, you can browse through them, read the important messages, and scan the others quickly. Messages sometimes have attachments in the form of document files, pictures, or other extra material. Outlook Express can display these files or save them to your hard disk drive.

View a Message

1. Click the Inbox shortcut on the Outlook Bar to see your incoming messages

2. Choose Layout from the View menu and select the Use Preview Pane check box to preview messages in a separate window.

3. Scan through your messages by selecting them and reading their contents in the preview pane at the lower-right side of the Outlook window.

4. To display a message in its own window, double-click the message.

5. Click the Next Item button to display the next message.

6. Click the Previous Item button to display the previous message.

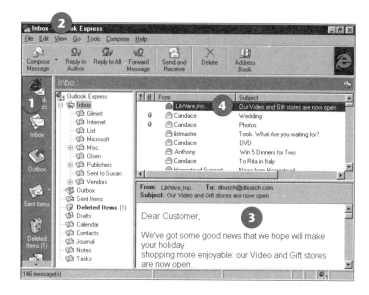

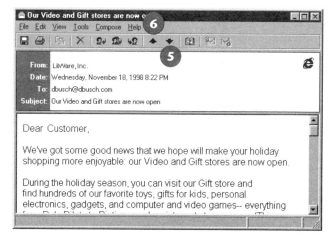

TIP

Save an attachment to your hard disk drive. *Right-click an attachment's icon at the bottom of the message window, and then choose Save As from the shortcut menu to store the attachment separately on your hard disk drive.*

TIP

View using Quick View. *If you want to view picture attachments in a separate window, install the Windows Quick View add-on attachment. Have your Microsoft Windows CD-ROM ready. Then click the Start button, point to Settings, and choose Control Panel. Double-click Add/Remove Programs, click the Windows Setup tab, and choose Accessories from the list. Click Details, click the Quick View check box, and then click OK.*

View a Message Attachment

1. Choose Options from the Tools menu.

2. Click the Read tab.

3. Click the Automatically Show Picture Attachments In Messages check box.

4. Click OK.

5. Select the message with the attachment.

6. View the picture in the preview pane.

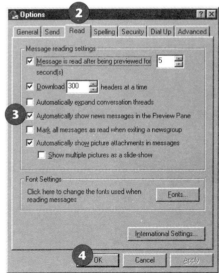

Replying to Messages

If you want to reply to a message you receive, all you need to do is click the Reply To Author or Reply To All button and add the text you want to send.

Reply to a Message

1. Display or select the message.

2. Click the Reply To Author button to reply to the sender only, or the Reply To All button to reply to all recipients of the message, including the sender.

3. Type your message.

4. Click the Send button to put the message in your Outbox.

5. Click the Send And Receive button when you're ready to send the message.

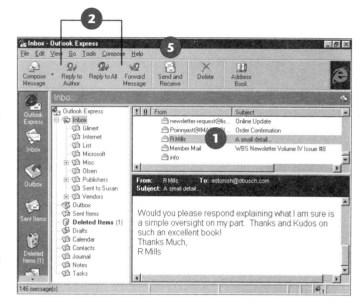

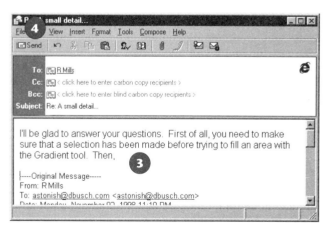

SEE ALSO

For information on forwarding to a distribution list, see "Working with Distribution Lists" on page 172.

SEE ALSO

For more information about sending messages, see "Composing and Sending E-Mail Messages" on page 168.

TIP

Reply to a message with an attachment. *When you reply to a message that contained an attachment, Outlook Express does not return the attachment to the sender. It simply appends a list of the files that were attached to the original message.*

Forward a Message

1. Select the message you want to forward to someone other than the original recipients.

2. Click the Forward Message button.

3. Type the e-mail address of the person to whom you want to forward the e-mail message in the To box, or click the To button to open the Address Book.

   ◆ If you're using the Address Book, click the OK button when you're finished adding addresses.

4. Type any new text you want to accompany the forwarded e-mail message.

5. Click the Send button to put the message in your Outbox.

6. Click the Send And Receive button when you're ready to send the message.

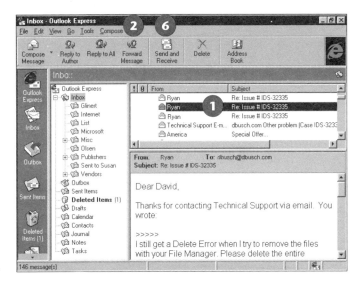

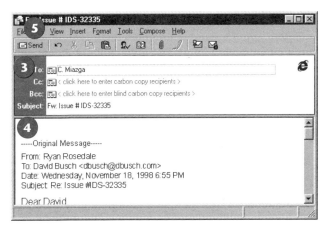

Composing and Sending E-Mail Messages

It's easy to send e-mail messages. All you really need is the e-mail address of your recipient. Outlook Express helps you by keeping a list of e-mail addresses in your Address Book and can help spice up your messages with *stationery*—preformatted message forms with graphics and color included, ready for your personalized text.

Create an E-Mail Message

1. Click the Compose Message button.

2. Type the e-mail address of the person you're sending the message to, or click the business card icon to choose a name from the Address Book.

3. When the Address Book appears, select a name from the scrolling list and click either the To, Cc, or Bcc button to add that address to the recipient list. You must have at least one address in the To line, but the others can remain blank.

4. Click OK when you are finished.

5. Optionally, add any other recipients by typing their e-mail addresses.

6. Type a description of your message in the Subject box.

7. Type your message text in the message area.

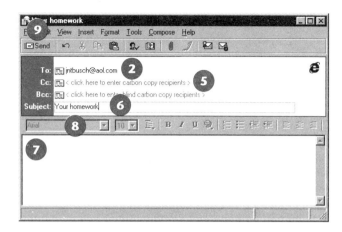

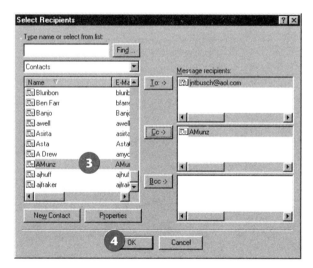

Use stationery. *Click the drop-down arrow next to the Compose Message button to choose from any of several predesigned stationery forms. Add your own text to these attractive forms. You can also save any message you create as stationery by selecting the message and choosing Save As Stationery from the File menu.*

Set default stationery. *If you decide you want to use a particular stationery form by default every time you create a message, choose Stationery from the Tools menu and click the Mail tab. Click the This Stationery button and then click the Select button to choose the stationery Outlook Express will use by default.*

Attach a file to a message. *You can send documents and pictures along with your e-mail messages. After you've composed your message, use the commands on the Insert menu to attach a picture, text file, or other material to your e-mail.*

⑧ Select any text you want to format and use the Formatting toolbar in the New Message window to apply fonts, font sizes, or other formatting.

⑨ Click the Send button to put the message in your Outbox.

⑩ Click the Send And Receive button when you're ready to send the message.

Send an E-Mail Message

① Drag any draft messages that you've composed for mailing at a later time that are not already in the Outbox folder to the Outbox folder.

② Click the Send And Receive button.

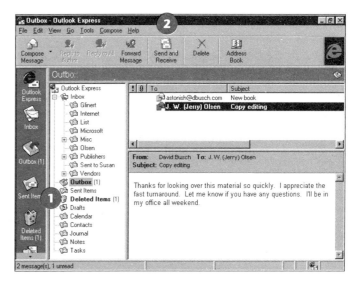

10

Adding Contacts to the Address Book

The Address Book is where you store e-mail addresses, making it easy to quickly address and send e-mail to lists of contacts, including individuals and entire groups that you define. You can also store a wealth of information about your contacts in the Address Book, including postal mail addresses, phone numbers, and other data.

Add a Contact

1. Click the Address Book button on the toolbar.

2. Click the New button on the Address Book's toolbar, and then choose New Contact.

3. Enter the name of the contact.

4. Enter an e-mail address for the contact.

5. Click Add.

6. Click the optional tabs, such as Home or Business, to add other information about the contact.

7. Click OK.

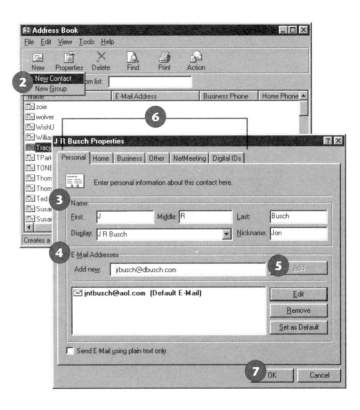

TIP

Find an address quickly.
When using the Address Book, type the first few characters of the name in the Type Name Or Select From List box to scroll to the name in your address list. Type just enough to narrow the search to a name or two on your list. For example, if you type "John Sm," the Address Book may show you listings for John Smith, John Smithers, and John Smythe.

TIP

Add notes to your contact information. *Right-click a contact and choose Properties from the shortcut menu that appears. Click the Other tab and add miscellaneous information about the contact in the space provided. You can include a birthday, a spouse's name, favorite foods, a college alma mater, or anything else you choose.*

TIP

Add incoming e-mail addresses to your Address Book. *If you receive mail from a new contact and want to add that person to your Address Book, display the message in its own window. Right-click the sender's address in the From box and choose Add To Address Book.*

Update a Contact

1. Click the Address Book button on the toolbar.

2. Click the Properties button on the Address Book's toolbar.

3. Edit any contact information you need to update.

4. Click OK.

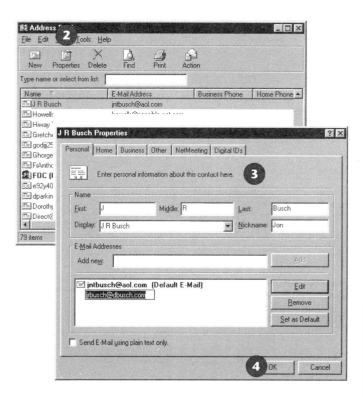

Working with Distribution Lists

You may want to send messages to a group of contacts without separately typing or selecting each of their e-mail addresses. For example, you might want to send personal news to a group of family members or business information to a select list of colleagues. Outlook Express allows you to create distribution lists in the form of contact groups. Just select a contact group instead of an individual e-mail address to send a message to everyone in the group.

Create a Contact Group

1 Click the Address Book button on the toolbar.

2 Click the New button on the Address Book's toolbar, and then choose New Group.

3 Type a name for the group.

4 Add members to the group.

◆ Click New Contact to type a new name and address.

◆ Click Select to choose highlighted existing contacts from the Address Book.

5 Click OK in the Select Group Members dialog box when you are finished.

6 Click OK in the Properties dialog box to save your new group.

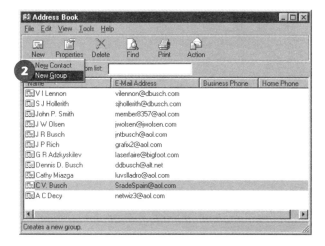

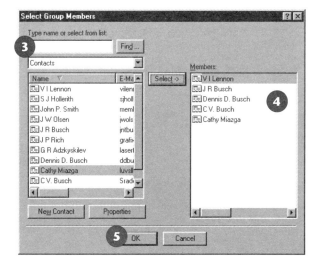

Categorize contacts using multiple distribution lists.

Use as many contact groups as you like to create useful categories. For example, you might want to group business associates into separate lists by department, or family members by the branch of the family tree they represent.

Add groups to groups.

When you create a new group, it can consist of any combination of one or more individuals and one or more groups. That is, groups can become part of a larger group. If you defined a group for each department in your company, you could also create a group called Whole Company that consists of each of the other groups.

Send Mail to a Distribution List

1. Click the Compose Message button on the toolbar.

2. Type the name of the distribution list you want to send the message to or click the business card icon to choose a distribution list from your Address Book.

   ◆ You can also add individuals to the recipient list.

3. If using the Address Book, click OK when you are finished adding distribution lists.

4. Type a description of your message in the Subject box.

5. Type your message text.

6. Select any text you want to format and use the Formatting toolbar in the New Message window to apply fonts, font sizes, or other formatting.

7. Click the Send button to put your message in your Outbox.

8. Click the Send And Receive button when you're ready to send the message.

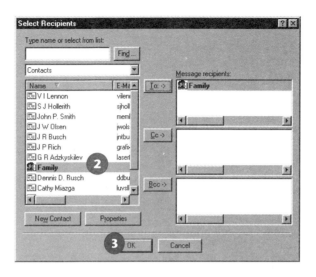

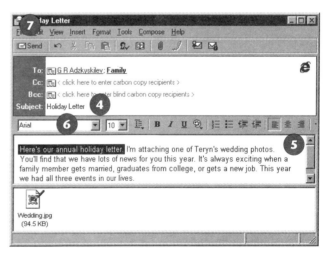

Filing Incoming and Outgoing Mail

While you may delete some mail immediately after reading it, you may want to keep other messages for reference. As you create drafts to send, you'll often want to temporarily store them in folders until it's time to e-mail them. Outlook Express can organize both incoming and outgoing mail in folders that you create. You can drag messages from your Inbox or another folder to your Outbox or any folder you want.

Create a Folder

1. Right-click the Inbox shortcut on the Outlook Bar.

2. Choose New Folder from the shortcut menu.

3. Type a name for the folder.

4. Choose the folder that the new subfolder should be placed in.

5. Click OK.

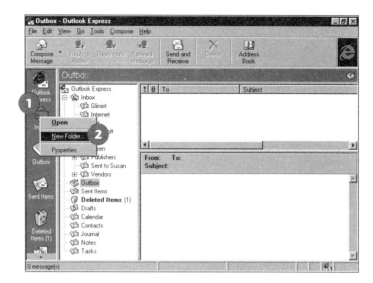

Create nested folders. *A good way to organize your messages is to create a series of nested folders. Create a folder called Personal for all your private mail, and define sub-folders within it for family, club, or recreation messages.*

Use a temporary trash can. *If you find that you sometimes need an item that you've deleted, create a new folder called Trash and place e-mail messages that you're not certain you will no longer need there. Outlook Express won't remove them until you move them to the Deleted Items folder.*

Put pending outgoing messages in the Drafts folder. *Deposit messages that aren't quite ready for delivery in the Drafts folder until you want to e-mail them.*

Store Mail in a Folder

1. Display the folder containing the item you want to move.

2. Right-click the message.

3. Choose Move To from the shortcut menu.

4. Select the folder to move the message to.

5. Click OK to move the message.

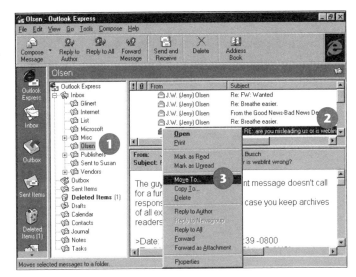

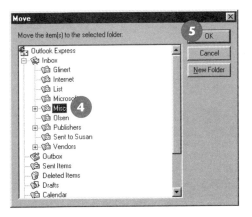

10

Printing Messages

Although you can keep e-mail messages stored in your Outlook Express folders for a long time, you may want to print some of them to file away. Or you may need to send a copy of a message by regular mail, or distribute it to someone in your office without using e-mail. Outlook Express has the same flexible printing options as the other Microsoft Works tools.

TIP

Print more than one message. *To print several messages consecutively, select them while pressing the Shift key (to specify adjacent messages) or while pressing the Ctrl key (to specify non-adjacent messages), and then right-click any of the messages and choose Print from the shortcut menu.*

Print a Message

1. Display or select the message.

2. Choose Print from the File menu.

3. Choose printing options, such as which printer to use or the number of copies.

4. Click OK.

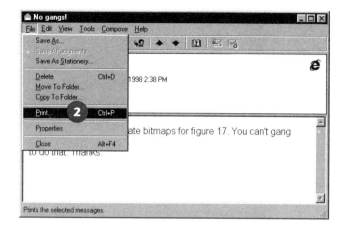

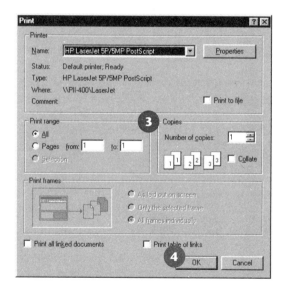

Preparing Cards with Graphics Studio Greetings 99

Microsoft Graphics Studio Greetings 99 is a versatile tool that allows you to create your own greeting cards to print or e-mail to friends and colleagues. You don't have to be an artist to produce attractive cards with Greetings. The application offers a rich collection of predesigned projects, complete with suggested messages and pictures. These projects make great foundations for creating personalized greetings in a hurry, or when you want some creative ideas from a professional designer.

Greetings produces several different kinds of projects. Paper projects are printable items such as announcements, greeting cards, invitations, and stationery. E-mail projects are greetings with optional animations and sounds that you can distribute using your Internet mail account. Occasions projects let you design cards for a long list of special events, such as Father's Day, Mother's Day, or Valentine's Day. You can select from a variety of themes for each kind of holiday or event. Microsoft Picture It! Express is included in Microsoft Works to help you create eye-catching pictures for your cards. You can use this tool to work with photos you already have or acquire images from scanners or digital cameras. You can touch up pictures, correct incorrect colors, or assemble several pictures into a collage.

Viewing the Greetings Window

Choose project categories.

Read about Greetings.

Choose the type of project.

Start a project from scratch.

Find projects on the Web.

Open one of your own projects.

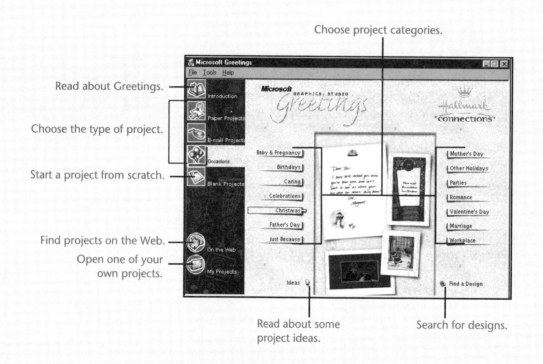

Read about some project ideas.

Search for designs.

Choosing a Predesigned Template

The fastest way to create a card is to use a predesigned template, which has all the elements, including pictures and suggested text, already in place. Once you've selected a template, a wizard leads you through selecting a theme and entering other basic information. Then you're free to customize your design.

TIP

Use preprinted paper. *The Hallmark Papers category allows you to create projects to print on colorful, preprinted paper from Hallmark.*

Choose a Template

1. Make sure the Greetings CD-ROM is inserted in your CD-ROM drive.

2. Click the Paper Projects icon.

3. Click a category, such as Announcements or Greeting Cards.

4. Click the Start With A Predesigned Project You Can Personalize check box.

5. Click the check box next to the kind of project you want to create.

6. Click the Next button and follow the rest of the instructions provided by the wizard.

   ◆ As the wizard progresses, click the Work On My Own Now button to skip the remaining customizing steps and work on your own.

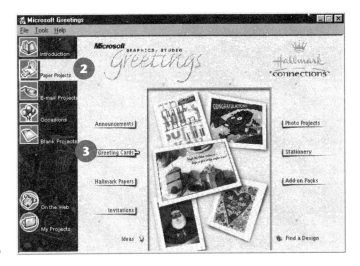

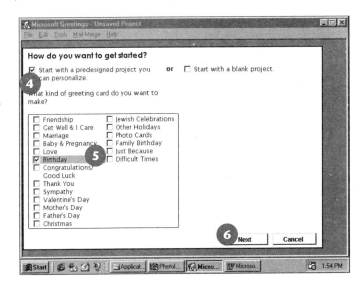

Viewing the Greetings Editing Window

Add a picture.

Add a shaped text block.

Add a text block.

Add a shape.

Add a straight line.

Add a freehand line.

Zoom in and out.

Edit the page.

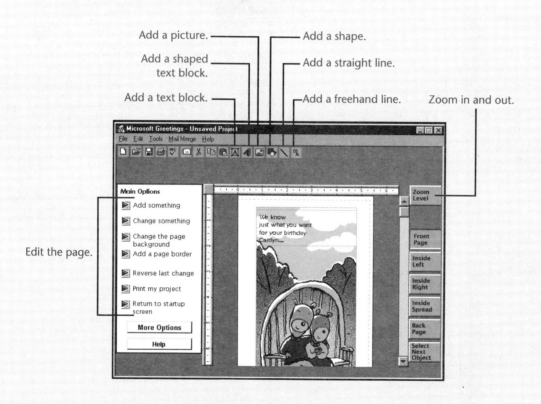

Main Options
- Add something
- Change something
- Change the page background
- Add a page border
- Reverse last change
- Print my project
- Return to startup screen

More Options

Help

Microsoft Greetings - Unsaved Project

File   Edit   Tools   Mail Merge   Help

We know just what you want for your birthday Caitlyn...

Zoom Level

Front Page

Inside Left

Inside Right

Inside Spread

Back Page

Select Next Object

Modifying a Project

Even if you allow the Greetings wizard to lead you through most of the steps to create a card, you'll still want to make changes before you're finished. You can change the text and add new objects, such as pictures included in the Clip Gallery or that you create yourself using a scanner, digital camera, or another digital image source.

> **TIP**
>
> **Add other objects.** *If you don't know exactly what you want to add, click Add Something and then click Something Else to have Greetings provide guidance.*

Modify a Project

1 Click the Add Something button to add text, pictures, shapes, or lines.

2 To modify an existing element, select it and click the Change Something button.

3 Click the Change The Page Background button to replace the background.

4 Click the Add A Page Border button to add a border around the edge.

5 Click the Reverse Last Change button to undo your last action.

6 Click the Print My Project button to print the project.

7 Click the Return To Startup Screen button to go the main screen.

8 Click the More Options button for more choices.

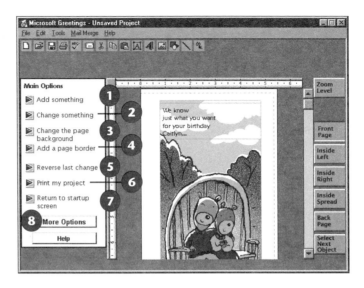

Entering or Editing Text

You can change the text in your message, rotate the text, or drag it around a page to position the text where you want it. When you add new text, Greetings automatically enlarges the text box to fit what you type.

TIP

Rotate in exact increments.
You can rotate a text block in exact increments. Click More Options in the Text Options window, choose Rotate, and select the increment you want.

Enter New Text

1. Click the Add New Text button.

2. Begin typing. Press the Enter key at the end of every line.

   ◆ To move the text block, move the insertion point to the edge of the text block until it changes into a cross shape with arrowheads, and then drag it.

   ◆ To resize a text block manually, drag one of the handles at the corners or midpoints of the text box's borders.

   ◆ To rotate a text block, drag the Rotation handle (which looks like a lollipop growing from the border of the text block).

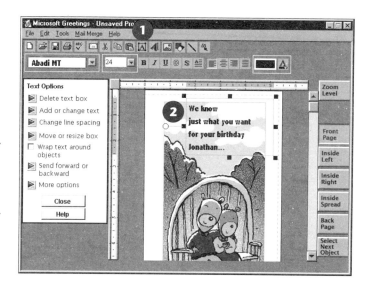

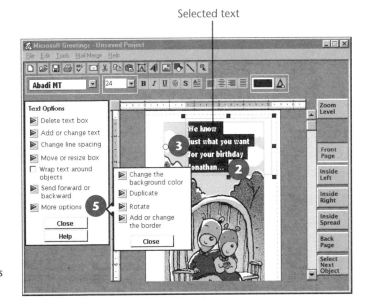
Selected text

Position text precisely. *The vertical and horizontal rulers can help you place text blocks exactly where you want them. If you want to use the rulers, make sure that they are active by choosing Rulers from the Tools menu.*

Add borders. *You can add a border consisting of thin or thick lines, or a fancy border suitable for a certificate or award.*

Edit Text

1. Place the insertion point inside the text block that you want to modify.

2. To add text, place the insertion point at the end of the current text.

3. To replace text, drag the insertion point to select the text you want to replace.

4. Type the text you want to add.

5. Click the Delete Text Box button in the Text Options window to remove an entire text block.

6. Click the More Options button if you want to change the text block's background color, add or change a border, or create a duplicate of the text.

11

Formatting Text

You can format text using fonts, applying special effects like outlining or boldfacing, and by setting the alignment. You can also choose any color of the rainbow for your text or its background. Line spacing can be set to single, 1.5 line, or double spacing, as well as any custom spacing between lines that you choose.

Specify Font, Size, and Style

1. Select the text you want to format.

2. Choose the font type from the Change Font Type drop-down list.

3. Choose the font size from the Change Font Size drop-down list.

4. Choose one or more boldface, italic, underline, outline, and shadow effects in any combination.

5. Click the Big First Letter button to create an enlarged first letter for your text block.

6. Click the Change Color button to choose a color for your text from a set of sample swatches.

   ◆ Click the More Colors button to view a larger array of colors.

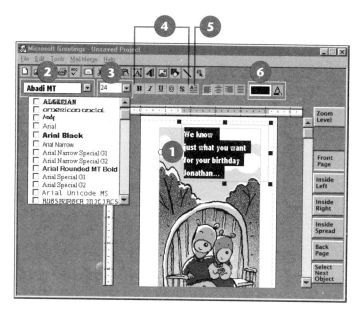

Stack text blocks. *To stack text blocks (or any objects) in front of or behind one another, select an object and click the Send Forward or Send Backward button. Then choose an option for moving the object forward or backward.*

Adjust line spacing visually. *Click the Change Line Spacing button in the Text Options window, and then click the up or down arrows next to the Or: Enter Custom Line Spacing In Points box and watch the line spacing change on the screen as you expand or contract the space between lines.*

View text close up. *Click the Zoom Level button at the right side of the screen to take a closer look at your text as you adjust font, line spacing, or other attributes.*

Align and Space Text

1 Select the text you want to align.

2 Click the Left Align, Center, Right Align, or Justified button to align the text.

3 Click the Change Line Spacing button to set single, 1.5 line, double spacing, or a custom spacing increment.

4 Click OK.

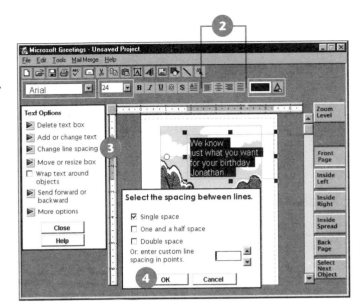

Adding Shaped Text and Other Objects

You can dress up your project with text that has been twisted, curved, slanted, or otherwise shaped into an interesting form. Creating shaped text is fun, because you can apply the text to a wavy curve, bend it around the perimeter of a circle, and add shadows, color, or shading to produce a humorous or festive look.

Add Shaped Text

1. Click the Add New Shaped Text button on the toolbar.

2. Type the text you want to shape.

3. Click the Change The Shape button to select a shape for the text.

4. Choose a shape.

5. Click the OK button to apply the shape to the text.

6. Choose any of the other option buttons to modify the font, style, alignment, rotation, color, or other attribute of the text.

7. Click the OK button when you are finished.

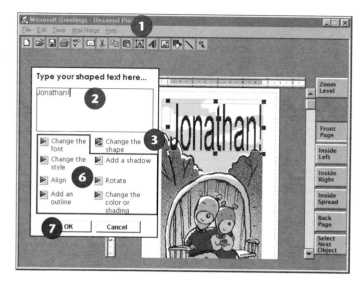

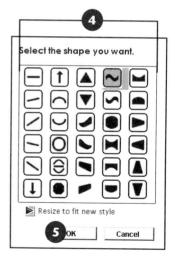

Group shapes. *To group shapes together so they can be treated as if they were a single object, click the first shape you want to group, and then hold down the Shift key and click additional shapes. Then click the Group button in the window that appears to combine them. To break the shapes apart, click the group to select it and then click the Ungroup button.*

Line up shapes. *To align shapes to one another, click the first shape you want to align, and then hold down the Shift key and click additional shapes. Then click the Line Up button in the window that appears, and choose how you want to align the objects. You can align them along their left, right, top, or bottom edges, or center them vertically or horizontally in relation to one another.*

Add Shapes or Lines

1. Click the Add New Shape button on the toolbar.

2. Click the shape you want.

3. Click the Add New Line button to add a straight line to the project.

4. Click the Draw My Own Line button to drag a freehand line with the mouse pointer.

5. Click the Flip Vertical or Flip Horizontal button if you want to flip your shape.

6. Choose line thickness and color, and add or remove arrowheads with the options on the toolbar.

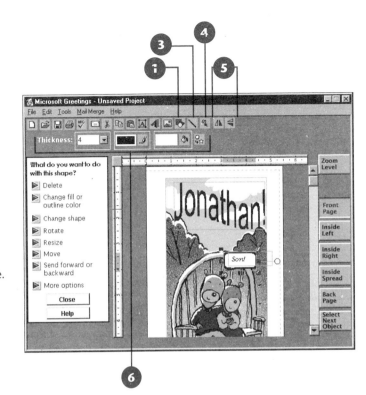

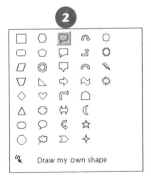

Adding Graphics

You can add graphics such as clip art or photographs to your project. Greetings includes an extensive Clip Gallery with a large stock of graphics that will dress up your cards. You can also add your own artwork or photographs. Clips that you want to use often can be placed in your own Favorites gallery, which you can access by choosing A Picture From The Clip Gallery from the Add Something window. You can browse categories for clips, or search for clips using keywords that describe them.

Add Artwork

1 Click the Add New Picture button on the toolbar.

2 Scroll through the list of categories and click the underlined link beneath a category you want to examine further.

3 Scroll through the clips in the gallery, and click one you want.

4 Choose an option from the shortcut menu.

- ◆ Choose Insert Clip to add the clip to your project.

- ◆ Choose Preview Clip to preview the clip in a separate window. (Greetings may tell you to insert a different CD-ROM that contains the clip you want.)

- ◆ Choose Add Clip To Favorites Or Other Category to place the clip in your Favorites gallery.

- ◆ Choose Find Similar Clips to locate other clips like the one you've selected.

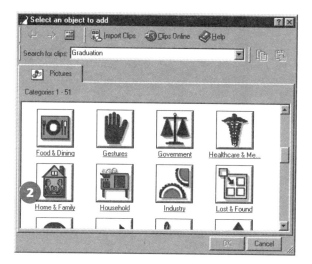

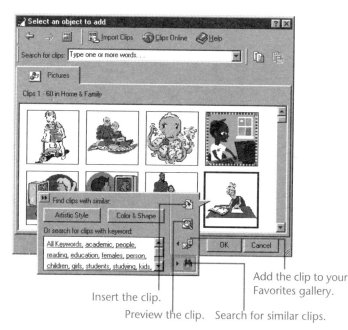

Insert the clip.

Preview the clip.

Add the clip to your Favorites gallery.

Search for similar clips.

TIP

Add clips to your gallery.
*Click the Import Clips button
in the Clip Gallery to find
other images you want to add
to your Clip Gallery.*

TIP

Search for clips. *To search
for relevant clips in the Clip
Gallery, type a keyword or two
in the Search For Clips box
and press the Enter key.*

SEE ALSO

*For information on working
with images, see "Editing
Pictures with Picture It! Express"
on page 194.*

Add a Photograph

1 Click Add Something on
the Main Options window
and then click A Picture
From Another Source.

2 Choose the type of picture
you want to add.

◆ Choose From Picture It!
Express Scan to scan
a picture.

◆ Choose From A Scanner
Or Digital Camera to
add a picture using
your scanner or digital
camera.

◆ Choose From My Com-
puter to browse your
computer's hard disk
drive to find a picture.

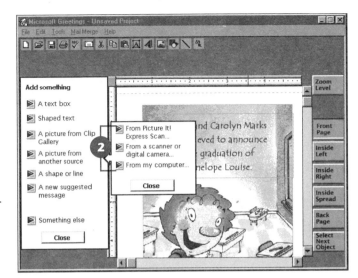

Adding Motion Clips

Projects created for e-mail can include sounds and animations that your recipient can enjoy when the message arrives. Greetings has its own collection of animations, but you can use any animated file in the GIF (Graphics Interchange Format) format.

Add a Motion Clip

1. Click the E-Mail Projects button at the main screen and follow the instructions to open an E-Mail Projects card.

2. On the Main Options window, click Add Something.

3. Click A Picture Or Animation From Clip Gallery.

4. Click the Motion Clips tab.

5. Click the underlined link beneath a category you want to examine further.

   ◆ You can search the available motion clips by typing keywords in the Search For Clips box and pressing the Enter key.

6. Browse through the motion clips in the gallery and click one that you want to work with.

7. Choose an option from the shortcut menu to insert a clip, play a preview, add the clip to your Favorites gallery, or to find similar clips.

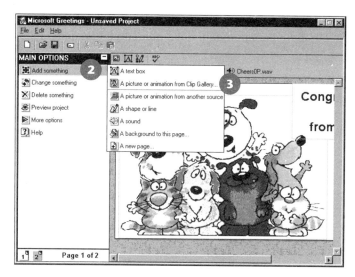

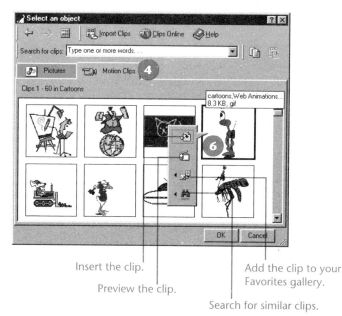

Insert the clip.

Preview the clip.

Add the clip to your Favorites gallery.

Search for similar clips.

Find clips online. *To locate additional clips on the Internet, connect to the Web, click Add Something on the Main Options window, choose A Picture Or Animation From The Clip Gallery, and then click the Clips Online button.*

Add a hyperlink to a clip. *You can add a hyperlink to a clip so when recipients of your e-mail click the clip in your message, they can jump directly to a Web page of your choice. Select the clip, choose Edit Animation from the Animation Options menu, and click Set Hyperlink. Then type the Web address you want to use as a link.*

Modify animation effects. *You can change how an animation first appears on the recipient's screen. Select the animation and choose Change Effects And Sounds from the Animation Options menu. Click the Entrance Effects button and choose an effect, such as Fade In or Checkerboard.*

Add a Motion Clip from Another Source

1. Click Add Something on the Main Options window, and then click A Picture Or Animation From Another Source.

2. Click From My Computer.

3. Explore your hard disk drive until you locate the animation clip you want to add.

4. Click the clip.

5. Click the Open button.

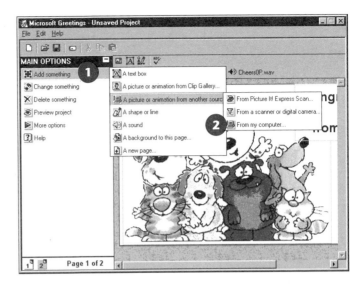

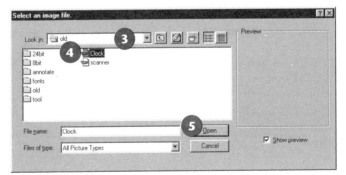

Adding Music and Sound Clips

You can add music and other sound clips to your e-mail project. Sounds can be attached to an object, such as a picture. The sound can play once or repeat as long as the object appears on the page. If a sound is attached to a page background, it will play once or as long as the page is displayed. Or you can attach a sound to an entire project, so it will play on all the pages of the project. You can also define a sound that will play when the e-mail recipient clicks the animated object.

Add a Sound Clip to a Background or a Project

1 Click the Change Something button on the Main Options window.

2 Click Background Effects And Sound.

3 Click the Sound Effects button.

4 Choose a sound from the list.

5 To add more sound choices, click the Add button.

6 Click a category in the Clip Gallery, click the sound you want to produce, and then click Insert Clip on the shortcut menu.

7 After inserting the clip, enter starting and stopping options for the clip, and whether it should repeat.

8 Click the OK button when you are finished.

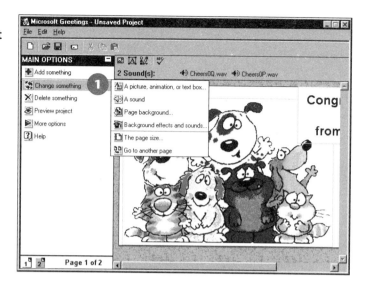

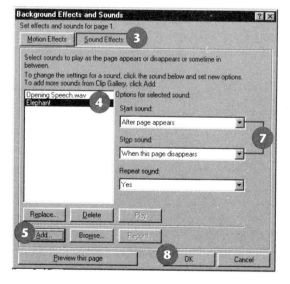

Add multiple sounds to an animation. *Select an animation and click the Change Effects And Sounds button on the window that appears. Click the Sound Effects button and add sounds, if required. Select the first sound and specify in the Start Sound drop-down list that it should play when the animation first appears. Select the second sound and schedule it to play after the animation appears. You can add a third sound by choosing To Begin After from the list and specifying a delay in seconds.*

Play a sound when the animation is clicked. *To have a sound play when the recipient of your e-mail message clicks the animation, select an animation and click the Change Effects And Sounds button. Click the Button Events button and then click the Play A Sound option button. Finally, click the Select Sound button to choose a sound from the Clip Gallery.*

Add a Sound Clip to an Object

① Select the object to which you want to attach the sound.

② Click the Change Effects And Sounds button in the Animation Options window.

③ Click the Sound Effects button.

④ Click the Add button.

⑤ Click a category in the Clip Gallery, click the sound you want to produce, and click Insert on the on the shortcut menu.

⑥ After inserting the clip, enter starting and stopping options for the clip, and whether it should repeat.

⑦ Click the OK button when you are finished.

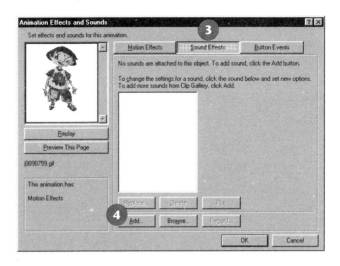

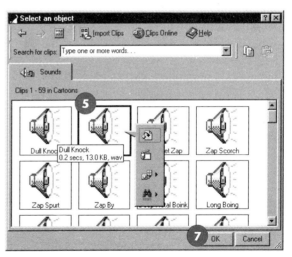

11

Editing Pictures with Picture It! Express

Even the best snapshots may need some corrections to make them look their best. Picture It! Express lets you adjust the brightness or contrast of a picture, increase the richness of the colors, or remove unpleasant off-color tones. If your photo subjects have red eyes, this stand-alone program can remove the red. If you want to add a soft edge to images, this tool will let you do that, too.

TIP

Rotate an entire collage.
To rotate all the pictures in a collage together, click the Size & Position button, click Rotate, and then click the Whole Picture tab. Enter the amount of rotation you want and click the Done button.

Open a Picture

1. Click the Get Picture button.

2. Click the My Picture button.

   ◆ Click the Scan Picture or Digital Camera button if you want to acquire a picture from a scanner or digital camera.

3. Navigate to the folder containing the pictures you want to work with.

4. Drag the pictures you want to use from the preview window to the filmstrip.

5. Click the Done button.

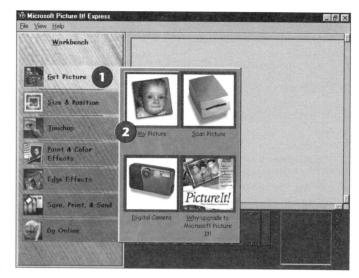

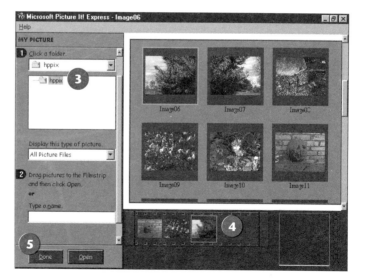

Change stacking order. *To change the order in which pictures are stacked in a collage with overlapping images, choose Stack from the View menu.*

Set the default path. *To set a default path that Picture It! will always use to look for your pictures, choose Options from the View menu, and then browse to or type a path in the Path To My Pictures box.*

Edit Pictures

1. On the filmstrip, double-click the picture you want to edit.

   ◆ To create a collage, drag one or more of the other pictures on the filmstrip onto the active picture area.

2. Select any picture in the collage by clicking it.

3. Drag any handle of a picture to resize it.

4. Drag the rotation handle (which looks like a lollipop) to rotate the picture in a freehand fashion.

5. To crop, rotate by a precise increment, flip, or change the stacking order of a picture, click the Size & Position button, and then choose the transformation you want. Click the Done button when you are finished.

6. Click the Save, Print & Send button to save the picture for use in Greetings or another program.

   ◆ You can also close the picture, print it, or save it as Windows wallpaper from the Save Print & Send menu.

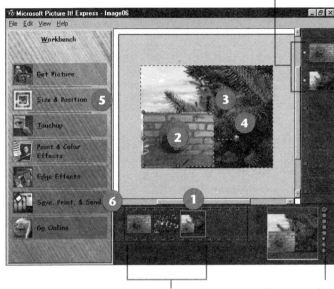

Drag to change stacking order.

Click to view other pictures on the filmstrip.

Drag to enlarge or reduce the magnification of the image view.

11

Correcting Pictures

Picture It! Express has the tools you need to correct slight defects in your photographs. For example, an unpleasant *red eye* effect can appear when the flash is positioned too close to the camera lens. The flash bounces off the retina of the subject's eyes directly back into the camera lens, producing a reddish effect. Or you may find that an image needs to be brightened or darkened. Picture It! can also adjust the contrast with convenient controls.

TIP

Fix red eye automatically.
Picture It! can fix red eye for you automatically. Click the Smart Task Fix button in the Fix Red Eye box. Then click inside each eye and click the Smart Task Fix button again. You may have to repeat the process to get rid of all the red eye.

Remove Red Eye

1 Click the Touchup button.

2 Click the Fix Red Eye button

3 Follow the directions for selecting the subject's eyes and removing unwanted red color.

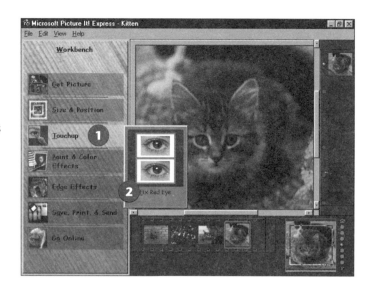

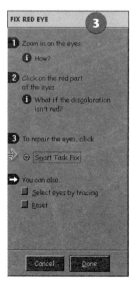

Adjust Brightness and Contrast

1. Click the Paint & Color Effects button.

2. Click the Brightness & Contrast button.

3. If your picture is a collage, click either the Object or Whole Picture tab, depending on whether you want to adjust only the selected object or the entire picture.

   ◆ If only one picture is on display, you can only adjust the whole picture.

4. Drag the yellow ball to adjust the richness of the colors.

5. Drag the blue ball toward the perimeter (to lighten) or back toward the center of the circle (to darken).

6. Drag the blue ball in a circle around the center of the disk to adjust contrast.

7. Click the Done button when you are finished.

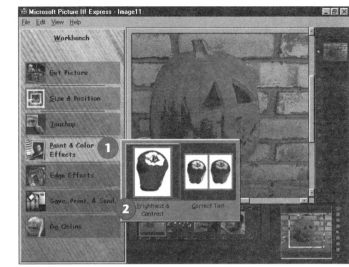

11

Adding Other Effects

You can change the color tint to remove many kinds of off-color tones in your pictures. For example, a face may be too red, and you'd like to adjust it to a more natural-looking color, or you may find that some grass has a distinctly magenta tone. There are two ways to accomplish this feat. You can find an area that is supposed to be white and let Picture It! alter the colors to make it neutral and without color cast. Or you can manually adjust color corrections until the image looks neutral.

TIP

Blend pictures. *Use the Soft Edges effect to blend together several pictures in a collage in an attractive way.*

Add an Effect

1. Click the Edge Effects button in the Workbench window and then click the Soft Edges button.

2. Drag the slider to soften or sharpen the edges of the photo.

3. Click Done.

4. Click the Paint & Color Effects button in the Workbench window.

5. Click Correct Tint.

6. Click the Object or Whole Picture tab, depending whether you want to adjust only the selected object in a collage or the entire picture.

7. Click a white area of the picture.

   ◆ If the picture has no white areas, drag the yellow ball on the edge of the rainbow-colored circle until the color of the image looks more neutral, and then click the + and – buttons to make fine-tuning adjustments.

8. Click Done when you are finished.

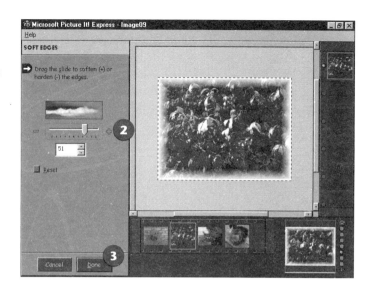

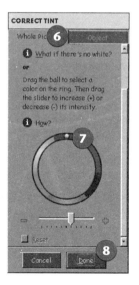

Microsoft Expedia Streets 98 is your gateway to a wealth of travel information. You can locate addresses, find the location of places even if you know nothing but the names of streets that intersect near it, or explore a region for points of interest. If you're planning a visit, Streets 98 can help you locate a hotel that meets your needs and budget, or a restaurant to fit your appetite. Streets 98 is also a great way to explore the United States by browsing through the maps and places of interest.

The Streets 98 database is large, so remember to keep the CD-ROM in your CD-ROM drive while you access the wealth of information it holds.

Traveling with Expedia Streets 98

Reading Expedia Streets Maps

View articles on hotels and restaurants, or search online.

Add a Pushpin.

View points of interest.

Highlight cities, towns, or points of interest.

Highlight a route.

Define an area of interest on the map.

Click to zoom in and out.

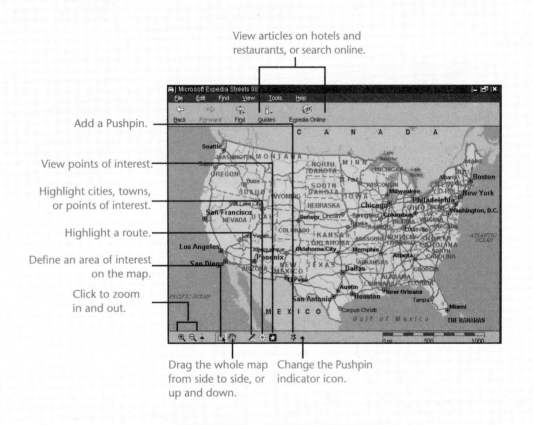

Drag the whole map from side to side, or up and down.

Change the Pushpin indicator icon.

Viewing a Map

If you don't have a specific place or address in mind, you can still enjoy exploring a map using Expedia Streets' tools. You can easily zoom in and out of a map, locate points of interest, add Push-pins to mark places you've found, or use a highlighter to trace a route. Annotate the places you find with tidbits of information to jog your memory when you revisit them later.

TIP

Adjust the radius of your search. *Drag the slider to increase or decrease the radius searched for points of interest.*

TIP

Mark routes. *You can use the Highlight tool to trace your route through a region during a vacation, business trip, or even repeated visits.*

Explore a Map

1. Click the Zoom Area button.

2. Click the map and hold down the mouse button and drag a rectangle around the area you want to view.

3. Click inside the rectangle you just drew to zoom in.

4. Click the Points Of Interest button.

5. Click the map to locate points of interest near that location.

6. Click the plus sign next to a category in the list of points of interest to expand the category.

7. Select a point of interest you want to know more about.

8. Click the Information button to read about that point.

9. Click the Close button to return to the list of points of information.

10. When you're finished examining the list, click the Close button.

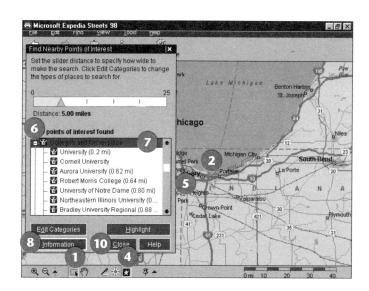

Finding a Place

You can quickly generate a map pointing to any exact location in the United States if you know the address, the cross streets (such as Maple and Washington Streets), or other information. The more facts you have on hand, the more likely Streets will be able to find the exact location you want. If your information is sketchy, Expedia can present you with a list of possible choices.

Find an Address

1. Click the Find button on the toolbar.

2. Choose An Address.

3. Type as much of the address as you know.

   ◆ If you don't know an exact address, you can type the nearest intersecting streets.

   ◆ If you don't know the city, state, or Zip code, leave any or all of those boxes blank.

4. Click the Find button.

5. If more than one location match the information you entered, choose the address you want from the list Expedia presents, and click OK.

6. Click the Zoom In and Zoom Out buttons or the Zoom slider to zoom the map view in or out.

7. Click OK when you are finished.

   ◆ You can also click Find New to begin a new search.

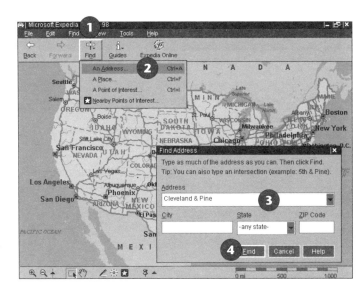

Zoom slider

Find a Place

1. Click the Find button on the toolbar.

2. Choose A Place.

3. Type as much of the place name as you know.

4. Choose a state, or choose Any State if you aren't sure which state the place is in.

5. Click the Find button to search.

6. If several locations match, choose the place you want from the list.

7. Click OK to view the place on the map.

8. Click the Zoom In and Zoom Out buttons or the Zoom slider to zoom the map view in or out.

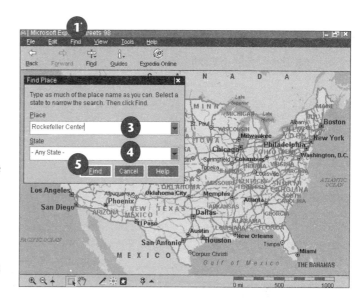

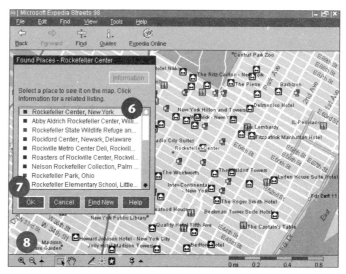

12

Locating a Restaurant

Expedia Streets 98 includes the huge ZAGATSURVEY Restaurants guide, with information on many of the best eating places in the United States. You can search its database to find restaurants by region, type of cuisine, or other amenities, such as decor. Although the reviews concentrate on better, full-service restaurants, you'll find the locations of your favorite fast-food and take-out places here, too.

Find a Restaurant by Region

1. Click the Guides button.

2. Click ZAGATSURVEY Restaurants.

3. Choose a region, type of cuisine, price and ratings categories, and any special criteria you may have.

4. Click the Find button.

5. Select the restaurant you want from the list.

6. Click the Information button to read about the restaurant.

7. Click the Locate or Highlight button if you want to find the address of the restaurant or mark it on the map.

8. Click the Close button when you're finished viewing the restaurant's information.

9. Click the Close button when you are finished searching for restaurants.

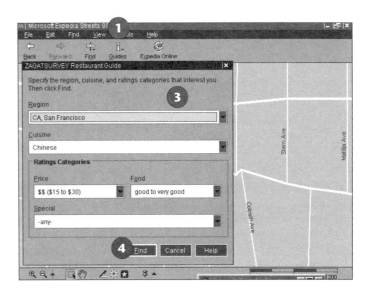

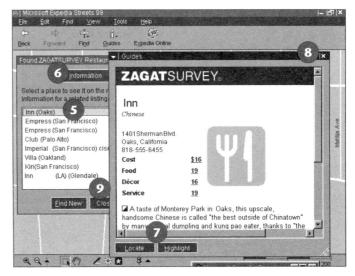

Annotate with Pushpins.

If you find a restaurant you really like, place a Pushpin on the map to mark it. Just click the Pushpin icon at the bottom of the screen, and click at the point on the map where you want to insert it. When the pin is placed, a label appears. Type a name for the pin in the label, and add any notes you want.

Store your annotations.

Choose Save Map from the File menu and give the map a name. You can load it at any time to view the Pushpins you've placed and read the annotations you've made.

Browse Restaurant Reviews

1 Click the Points Of Interest button.

2 Click a point on the map where you'd like to search for restaurants.

3 Scroll to the category of restaurant you want.

4 Click the plus sign next to a category to see all the restaurants in that category.

5 Select a restaurant.

6 Click the Information button to read about that restaurant.

7 Click the Locate or Highlight button if you want to find the address of the restaurant or mark it on the map.

8 Click the Close button when you're finished viewing the restaurant's information.

9 Click the Close button when you are finished searching for restaurants.

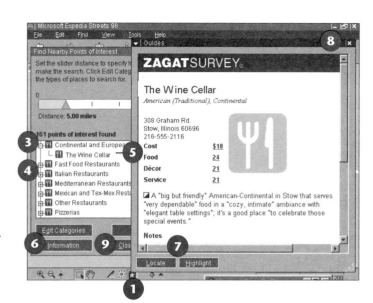

Finding a Hotel

Planning ahead for a place to stay can be one of the most important parts of mapping a trip. Streets 98 includes information on more than 13,000 hotels, motels, bed-and-breakfast inns, and other accommodations. Use the database to find the hotel that suits you and, if you like, go online to the Expedia Web site to make your reservation over the Internet.

TIP

Lock in a price. *Keep in mind that the prices shown in Streets 98 are subject to change on a seasonal basis. Use the Expedia Web site to make reservations as soon as you know you'll be traveling. You'll not only find out the price you'll pay, but can make a guaranteed reservation that will be held until your arrival.*

Locate a Hotel

1. Click the Guides button.

2. Choose Expedia Hotel Directory.

3. Specify the type of accommodations you want.

4. Click the Find button.

5. Scroll through the list of hotels and select one to read about.

6. Click the Information button to read about that hotel.

7. If the Online Reservations Button appears, click it to make a reservation by using the Expedia Web site.

8. Click the Close button when you are finished reading about a hotel.

9. Click the Close button when you are done searching for hotels.

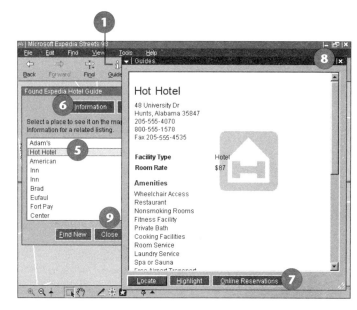

Managing Your Finances with Money 99 Basic

If you've used a conventional checkbook and register and can operate a calculator, you can use Microsoft Money 99 Basic. However, Money 99 can do much more than either of these familiar tools. It can help you manage your budget, provide the information you need to make sound financial decisions, and track investments. Best of all, Money combines the information from several different accounts to provide a helpful overview of your finances, and assists in planning your retirement, preparing taxes, and avoiding many common mistakes.

Whether you're planning to pay for college for yourself or your children, trying to decide whether to refinance a mortgage, tracking your net worth, or just interested in keeping a balanced checkbook, Money 99 Basic has all the features you need. For this chapter, I assume you have installed Money 99 Basic, and know how to start it from the Start menu.

Viewing the Money
Home Screen

Click to move backward
through the windows
you've recently visited.

Click to return to this home page.

Click to view
your accounts.

Choose menu commands.

Click for audio help.

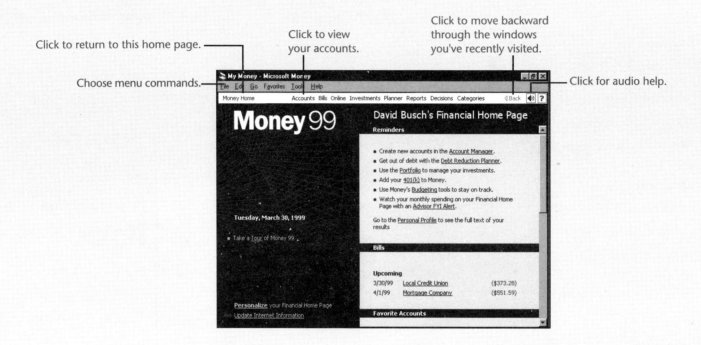

Managing Finances

Managing your finances is simple with Microsoft Money 99 at your fingertips to collect information, provide accurate tallies, and display reports that show where your money is going. Although Money's features cover a broad range of financial matters, they can all be accessed quickly with easy-to-use icons, buttons, and menus.

Microsoft Money stores information about your finances in collections called *files*. Each file includes information about one individual or small business and can include several different bank accounts, charge cards, or investment plans. For example, you could create one file that tracks all your personal accounts and investments, and a second one for all the accounts related to your small business. By allocating information about accounts in files, Money makes it easy to group your records appropriately.

The core of your financial management system is careful budgeting, built around Money's computerized checkbook. Instead of keeping track of your checks and deposits in a paper register, you can enter and view this information in an on-screen register, specifying income and expense categories of your choice for every entry. That means that Money can balance your checkbook, and show exactly how much you spend for each classification. You can transmit payments electronically over the Internet, or print your own checks, too. On the basis of its checkbook features alone, Money can save you a great deal of time.

Tracking credit card purchases and payments can be as important for budgeting as keeping detailed checking records, but few people bother to do so because of the time involved. Money makes entering and keeping these records as easy as working with a check register, so you're more likely to make credit card expenditures wisely.

Making sound financial decisions is another crucial aspect of personal finance. You'll want to plan carefully for your retirement, evaluate your investment and savings plans, and follow your tax deductions. If you invest in real estate or manage a small business, you'll want to watch where the money comes from and where it goes just as closely as if you managed a giant conglomerate. The key is to collect every bit of information in a form that is accessible and makes sense to you. In personal finance, too little knowledge can be a dangerous thing.

Creating and Opening Money Files

Money can keep track of financial matters for several different people, so everyone in your family can create his or her own personal file of information. You might want to allow your children to manage their own finances with files of their own, or create separate files for individual businesses you operate. Each file keeps a list of accounts, their balances, and every transaction you enter into Money. You can easily create several files for yourself (say, one for your personal expenses and one for a business), and switch back and forth between files. To start Money, just point to the Start Menu, point to Programs, and choose Microsoft Money.

Create a New Money File

1 Choose New from the File menu.

2 Enter a name for the file in the File Name text box.

3 Click OK.

◆ Choose to back up the file, if you wish, when asked.

4 Fill out the forms with the personal information requested, scrolling down the list as required.

5 Click the Done Answering Questions button when you are finished, and then click the Done button on the Action Plan screen.

6 When the Money home screen appears, click the Set Up Your Accounts link to begin creating accounts within that Money file.

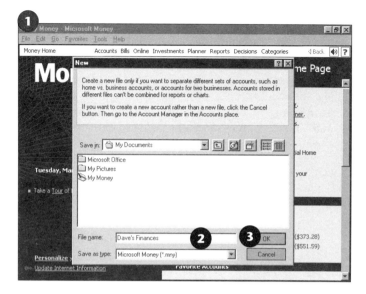

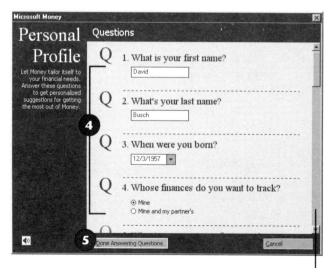

Scroll down to see all the questions.

SEE ALSO

For information on setting up accounts in a new Money file, see "Setting Up Bank Accounts" on page 214 and "Setting Up Credit Card Accounts" on page 216.

SEE ALSO

For information on importing Quicken files into a new Money file, see "Importing Files from Quicken" on page 212.

TIP

Display one file. *Money can display only one file at a time. When you open a new file, any other open file is closed. Money will offer to back up the file for you, either to a floppy disk or to your hard disk drive, as you prefer.*

Open an Existing Money File

1. Choose Open from the File menu.

2. Click the Look In drop-down arrow and locate the drive and folder where your Money file is stored.

3. Double-click the Money file to open it.

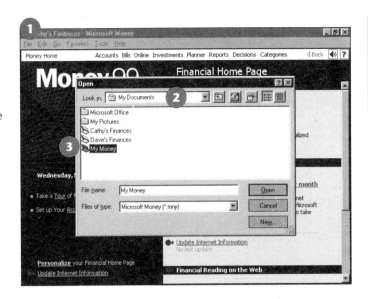

Importing Files from Quicken

If you or some member of your family have checkbook files stored in Quicken format, you can import them so you can combine all your accounts in Money. The Converter Wizard For Quicken leads you through all the steps needed to import these files. All you need to know is where the files are located. Money creates a duplicate file in its own format, so the original files remain intact.

TIP

Retain your favorite budget. *Money supports only one active budget, and converts the one most recently used by Quicken. To make sure your favorite budget is active after the conversion, open the Quicken file and use the favorite budget just before you convert the file.*

Import a File from Quicken

1. Choose Convert Quicken File from the File menu.

2. Click the Look In drop-down arrow and locate the drive and folder where the Quicken file is located.

3. Double-click the Quicken file to start the Converter Wizard For Quicken.

4. Follow the wizard's instructions, clicking the Next button as required and filling in the requested information.

5. When you're done with the wizard, click Finish.

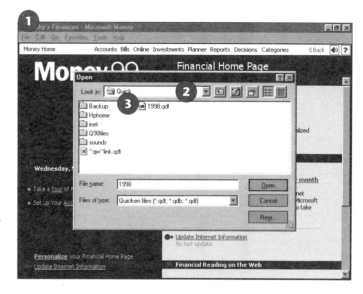

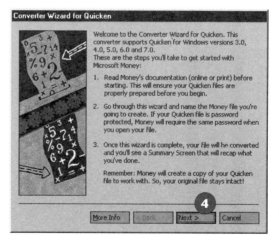

Archiving a Money File

Each time you close a file, Money asks if you'd like to make a backup, either to your hard disk or to a floppy disk. Frequent backups are your best protection against losing data. As an added safeguard, Money offers a simple way to archive files. An *archive* is a file that contains selected transactions that you elect to remove from your working file. The old records are still available in the archive if you need them, but your main file is smaller and easier to work with. Archives also provide an additional level of backup protection if your computer fails.

TIP

Access archives. *You can access an archive in the same way as a regular Money file, by choosing Open from the File menu. Navigate to your archive's location, select it, and click the OK button.*

Archive a Money File

1. Choose Archive from the File menu.

2. Enter a cut-off date before which you want to include transactions in the archive.

3. Click the OK button.

4. Enter a name for the backup file, or accept the default name Money suggests.

5. Click the OK button.

6. Indicate which types of files you want removed from each of your Money accounts.

7. Click the OK button when you are finished.

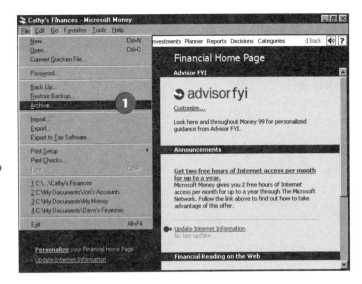

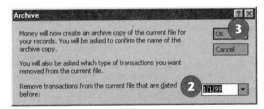

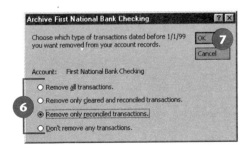

Setting Up Bank Accounts

Once you have created or opened a file, you can set up a separate account for each bank account that you want to track with Money. Once you've opened the account, you can enter checks and deposits into an on-screen register that looks much like the paper registers you're accustomed to. All you need to know to set up a bank account is the name of the bank and the most recent balance. You can enter other details, such as the account number, later if you like.

Create a New Account

1. Click Accounts on the navigation bar to reveal the Account Manager.

2. Click the New Account button.

3. Choose either a bank account or an account that is not held at a bank, brokerage, or other financial institution, and click the Next button.

4. Choose the type of account you want to set up, and click the Next button to begin the wizard.

5. Follow the instructions and fill in the information requested for account name, category, account number, and ending balance.

6. If you have no other accounts to set up for this institution, click the I Have No Other Accounts button, and then click the Next button.

7. Click the Finish button.

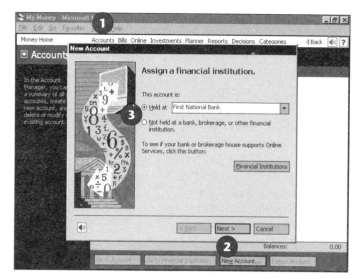

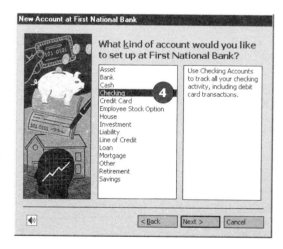

Add Account Information

1. Click Accounts on the navigation bar to reveal the Account Manager.

2. Right-click the account you want to modify and chose Go To Details from the shortcut menu.

3. Make any changes you like.

4. If desired, enter notes to yourself in the Comment box.

5. Click the Account Manager button when you are finished.

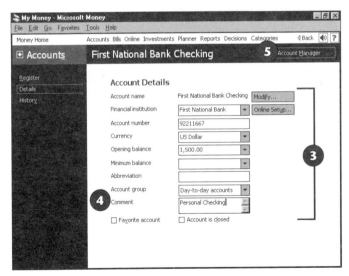

Setting Up Credit Card Accounts

Credit card accounts can be set up as easily as bank accounts by using the New Account Wizard. You'll need to know the name of the institution, your current balance owed, credit limit, and other details. If you like, you can make the payment on a credit card account a *recurring payment* (one that is repeated over time).

Create a New Account

1. Click Accounts on the navigation bar, if necessary, to show the Account Manager window, and then click the New Account button.

2. Fill in the name of the financial institution issuing the card.

3. Select Credit Card from the list.

4. Enter a name for the account or accept the name Money suggests.

5. Enter your account number.

6. Enter the account balance, if any.

7. Specify whether the card is a credit card or debit card.

8. If entering a credit card, enter the interest rate.

9. Enter the credit limit, if any.

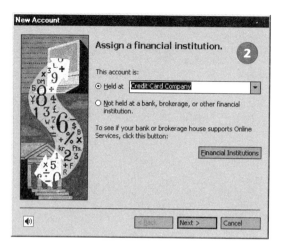

SEE ALSO

For information on setting up recurring payments, see "Entering Recurring Transactions" on page 224.

TIP

Specify a charge card. *If you have a card that must be paid off each month, specify Charge Card when asked by the wizard. And regardless of what kind of card you have, you can check the Always Pay Entire Balance Each Month check box if you want to pay in full each month.*

TIP

Manage introductory rates. *Money allows you to enter both an introductory interest rate and permanent interest rate. You can specify in the New Account Wizard when the permanent rate kicks in, so you'll always be able to track your credit card interest accurately.*

10 Click the Keep Track of Individual Credit Card Charges option button.

11 When the wizard is finished, click the I Have No Other Accounts At This Institution, and then click Next.

12 Click the Finish button.

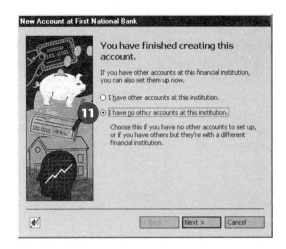

Recording a Deposit

You must enter the deposits you make on a regular basis to keep your check register current. Money allows you to enter deposits, categorize them according to income source, as well as enter memos to yourself so you will remember more about where the funds came from or where you have them earmarked. When you make a deposit, Money recalculates your bank balance.

SEE ALSO

For information on recording regular direct deposits, see "Entering Recurring Transactions" on page 224.

SEE ALSO

For information on splitting a deposit that consists of several items from different sources, see "Splitting Transactions" on page 222.

Record a Deposit

1. Click Accounts on the navigation bar, if necessary, to view the Account Manager.

2. Right-click the account you want to work with and choose Go To Register.

3. In the register, click the Deposit tab.

4. If necessary, click the New button.

5. Enter a deposit or check number if desired.

6. Enter the deposit date.

7. Enter the deposit amount.

8. Enter the name of the payor.

9. Click the drop-down arrow in the Category box and choose an income category.

10. Enter any memo you want for the deposit.

11. Click the Enter button to record the deposit.

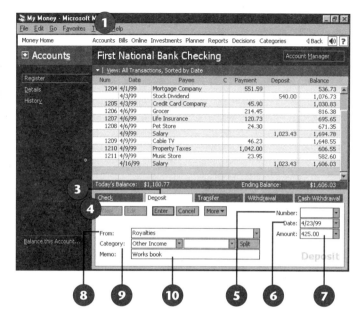

Recording a Paycheck

For many, paychecks will make up the majority of regular income. Money's handy Paycheck Wizard makes it simple to enter paychecks and list all the deductions and taxes so you can track gross and net income. You can monitor federal, state, and local income taxes; health insurance deductions; and your contributions to retirement plans. While recording a paycheck is a lot like recording other kinds of deposits, you don't have to fill in the amount immediately. The Paycheck Wizard allows you to enter all the amounts for wages and deductions, and then calculates and inserts the correct amount for you.

SEE ALSO
For information on making a paycheck a recurring transaction, see "Entering Recurring Transactions" on page 224.

Record a Paycheck

1. Click Accounts, if necessary, to view the Account Manager.

2. Right-click the account you want to work with and choose Go To Register.

3. In the bank account's register, click the Deposit tab.

4. Click New, if necessary.

5. Enter the deposit date.

6. Enter the name of your employer in the From field.

7. Type **Paycheck** in the Category box and press Tab to launch the Paycheck Wizard.

8. Follow the instructions offered by the wizard to enter gross wages, deductions, taxes, and other information.

9. Click Done when you are finished with the wizard.

10. Click Enter to record the paycheck.

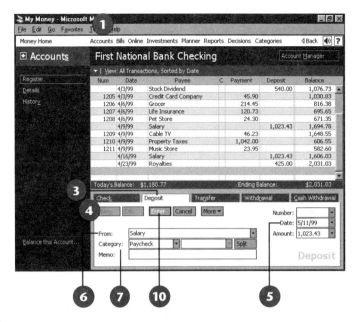

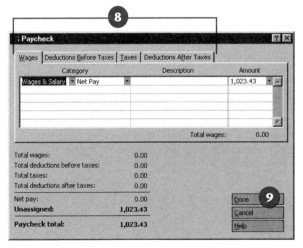

Recording Expenses

For Money's purposes, expenses include all the checks you write as well as any automatic teller machine (ATM) withdrawals you make, but don't include individual cash expenditures. You can record these debit items in the register the same way you enter deposits.

TIP

Use subcategories.
Subcategories allow you to track your expenditures more closely, especially if you have many expenses in a particular category. For example, if you play golf and tennis at separate clubs, you can keep track of dues, fees, lessons, and other expenses for each in Golf and Tennis subcategories created under a main Recreation category. That way, you can create a report tracking all your recreation expenses or only golf or tennis, as you prefer.

Enter a Check

1 Click Accounts, if necessary, to view the Account Manager.

2 Right-click the account you want to work with and choose Go To Register.

3 Click the Check tab, and click New if necessary.

4 Enter the check number.

5 Enter the check date.

6 Enter the check amount.

7 Enter the name of the payee.

8 Click the drop-down arrow in the Category field and choose an expense category.

9 Click the Enter button to record the check.

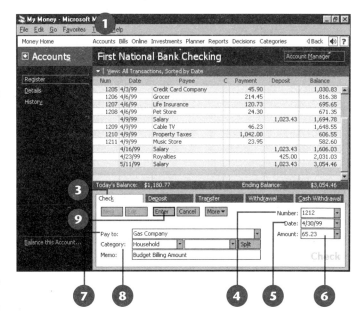

Create categories. *Although Money provides typical categories you can use to classify deposits and payments, you can easily set up your own categories. Click Categories on the navigation bar to view a list of the current categories. Click the New, Move, or Modify button to add a category, move a subcategory to a different location, or to change the name or category type (Expense or Income) of an existing category. To edit a category's details, select the category and click the Go To Category button. Enter your changes and click the Categories & Payees button when you are finished.*

SEE ALSO

For information on examining your expenses with reports, see "Creating Reports" on page 231.

Enter an ATM Withdrawal

① Click Accounts, if necessary, to view the Account Manager.

② Right-click the account you want to work with and choose Go To Register.

③ Click the Cash Withdrawal tab.

④ Click New if necessary.

⑤ Enter the withdrawal date.

⑥ Enter the withdrawal amount.

⑦ Click the drop-down arrow in the Category field and choose an expense category.

⑧ Enter a memo to yourself to describe the withdrawal.

⑨ Click the Enter button to record the withdrawal.

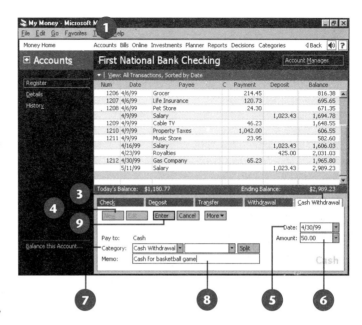

Splitting Transactions

Frequently, a bank deposit will contain checks from several payors, or include a mix of cash, checks, or money orders. You can split a deposit transaction and specify the source of each form of income if you like. Similarly, if you write a single check to cover multiple purchases from a vendor (such as both groceries and prescriptions), you can split that transaction to help keep track of where your money went.

TIP

Examine your categories.
If you find yourself splitting transactions frequently, examine the categories you've set up to make sure you have enough expense and income categories to classify your financial transactions.

Divide a Transaction

1. Click Accounts on the navigation bar, if necessary, to view the Account Manager.

2. Right-click the account you want to work with and choose Go To Register.

3. Right-click the transaction you want to split and choose Split from the shortcut menu.

4. Enter the first category on the first line.

   ◆ Enter a subcategory for that purchase or income if you like.

   ◆ Enter a memo to describe the category if you like.

5. Enter the amount spent or received for this category.

6. Repeat steps 4 and 5 for additional categories and subcategories.

7. Click the Done button when you are finished.

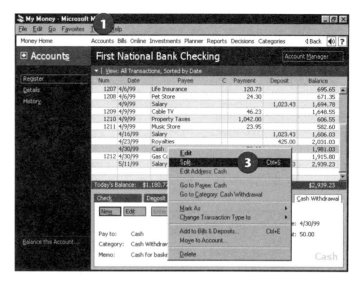

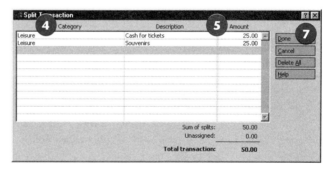

Correcting Errors

Mistakes happen. You can reverse them by fixing any errors you made when entering checks, deposits, or other transactions. Money allows you to edit a transaction at any time.

SEE ALSO

For information on reconciling and balancing your bank accounts, see "Reconciling Accounts" on page 228.

Fix an Error

1 Right-click the transaction you want to correct or modify.

◆ Choose Delete from the shortcut menu to remove the transaction.

◆ Point to Mark As and choose Void to void a transaction without deleting it entirely.

◆ Point to Change Transaction Type To in order to change to check, deposit, transfer, withdrawal, or cash withdrawal transactions.

◆ Choose Edit to modify the transaction. Click the field you want to edit. Enter your corrections. Click the Enter button when you are finished.

◆ Click Move To Account to switch the transaction to a different account.

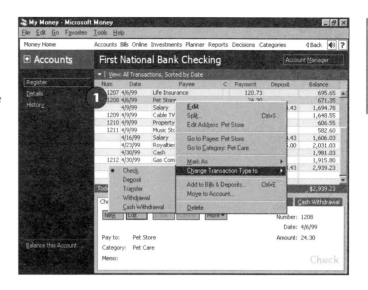

Entering Recurring Transactions

Money can keep track of when automatic payments are due and direct deposits are made so you don't have to watch the calendar closely. It can also track repeating bills such as utility payments and provide a reminder so you won't forget to pay them.

Add a Recurring Payment

1. Click Bills on the navigation bar.

2. Click the New button.

3. Click the Bill option button and click Next.

4. Click the More Than Once, At Regular Intervals option button.

5. Follow the wizard's instructions to enter information about the recurring payment, clicking Next after you've finished each screen.

    ◆ Choose the frequency of the recurring transaction from the Frequency drop-down list.

    ◆ Enter the payment details, including payee, amount, and categories.

    ◆ Choose a payment plan, and whether the payment is the same each time.

    ◆ Choose whether to record the first payment now.

    ◆ Click Finish when you are done.

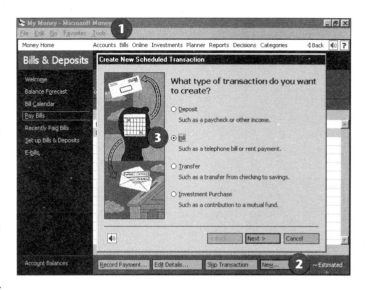

Use reminders. *Money will let you know 10 days before a bill is due. You can set a different reminder time by choosing Options from the Tools tab, clicking the Bills tab, and typing the number of days in advance of the due date.*

Make an existing transaction recurring. *To change an existing transaction into a repeating one, right-click the transaction in the register and choose Add To Bills & Deposits from the shortcut menu. Then enter the information for a recurring deposit or bill by using the Create New Scheduled Payment or Create New Scheduled Deposit wizards.*

Add a Recurring Deposit

① Click Bills on the navigation bar.

② Click the New button.

③ Click the Deposit option button and click Next.

④ Click the More Than Once, At Regular Intervals option button.

⑤ Follow the wizard's instructions to enter information about the recurring deposits, clicking Next after you've finished each screen.

◆ Choose the frequency of the transaction from the Frequencey drop-down list.

◆ Enter the deposit details.

◆ Enter the payment method.

◆ Specify whether the deposit is always the same amount

◆ Choose whether to record the first payment now.

◆ Click Finish when you're done.

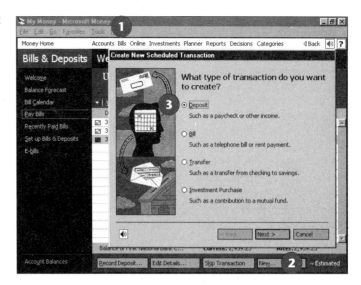

Finding Transactions

You can locate a transaction or find groups of transactions that meet search criteria you specify. Perhaps you entered a transaction into the wrong account, or spelled the name of the payor or payee incorrectly. Money can search by text you enter, category, date or date range, or amount so that you can quickly locate that "lost" transaction.

TIP

Use the Date tab. *The Date tab is useful when you aren't sure when you entered a transaction. You can specify a range of dates and search only for transactions that fall within those dates, such as December 1 through December 31 of the current year.*

Find a Transaction

1 Choose Find And Replace from the Tools menu to start the Find And Replace Wizard.

2 For a basic search, click the Simple Search option button.

◆ From the Search Across drop-down list, choose whether you want regular accounts or loan accounts searched.

◆ Enter the text you want to find in the Find This Text box.

◆ Choose which fields you want to search from the In This Field drop-down list.

◆ Click Next to start a simple search, finishing the procedure.

3 For an advanced search, click the Advanced Search button and carry out the following additional steps.

4 Click Next.

5 For both regular and loan accounts, select any or all of the tabbed options.

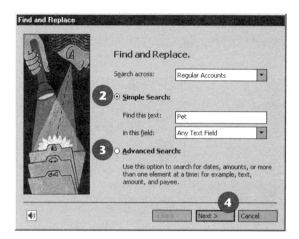

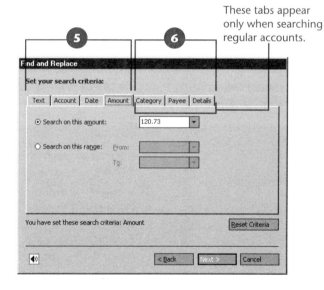

These tabs appear only when searching regular accounts.

TIP

Search for memos. *If you enter Memo information regularly, you can use those notes to search for a transaction with the Text tab. Perhaps you entered "Dinner with Client" and don't remember the date, amount, or even the restaurant where the dinner took place. Searching for the memo text can help you pinpoint the expenditure quickly.*

TIP

Find all checks to a payee. *Searching by payee is a quick way to produce a list of all the checks written to a particular individual or organization.*

TIP

Locate transactions posted to wrong accounts. *One of the most common errors is to enter a transaction into the wrong account. You may have two checking accounts, or more than one credit card account. In such cases, it's easy to post a transaction in a similar account. Money can search all your regular accounts or loan accounts to find misposted transactions.*

◆ Click the Text tab to locate transactions with specific text.

◆ Click the Account tab to choose which accounts to search.

◆ Click the Date tab to choose a date range.

◆ Click the Amount tab to search for a specific amount or range of amounts.

◆ Click the Category tab to find a transaction by category.

6 If you're searching regular accounts, choose any or all of the additional options.

◆ Click the Category tab to search a specific category

◆ Click the Payee tab to find a transaction by the name of the payee.

◆ Click the Details tab to find a transaction by other details.

7 Click Next to locate the transactions.

Results of search

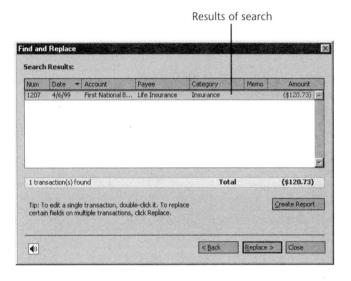

Reconciling Accounts

If you're using a paper register, the most difficult task you face each month may be reconciling and balancing your accounts. It's easy to enter a wrong figure into a register or forget to enter a transaction entirely. Matching returned checks with register entries can be tedious. While Money can't eliminate human error, its computerized register reduces mistakes and makes them easier to find if they do occur.

Reconcile Accounts

1. Click Accounts on the navigation bar to reveal the Account Manager.

2. Double-click the account you want to reconcile.

3. Click Balance This Account on the Accounts bar.

4. Click Next to advance beyond the introduction.

5. Enter the bank statement ending date in the Statement Date field.

6. Enter the starting balance in the Starting Balance field.

7. Enter the closing balance in the Ending Balance field.

8. Enter any service charges and choose a category for them.

9. Enter any interest received in the Interest Earned field, and categorize it.

10. Click Next.

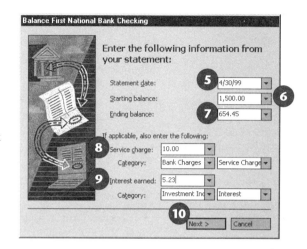

Find those errors. *If you're unable to reconcile your account, check for one of the following errors: a transaction amount that was entered incorrectly in your register; transactions that you neglected to enter in your register; transactions incorrectly marked as cleared or not cleared; checks entered as deposits, or deposits entered as checks.*

Reconcile an account. *If you can't find your error and want to balance your account, click Next when you are finished with the wizard and click the Automatically Adjust The Account Balance option button in the screen that appears. Money will create a cleared transaction for an amount that will make your statement balance.*

For more information on correcting mistakes in your register, see "Correcting Errors" on page 223.

11 Mark the checks and deposits that have cleared the bank.

◆ Click the C (cleared) column for all checks and withdrawals on your statement.

◆ Click the C (cleared) column for all deposits on your statement.

12 When the difference between the cleared balance and statement balance equals zero, as shown in the Try To Get Balance Difference To Zero area of the Accounts bar, click Next.

13 Click Finish when you are done.

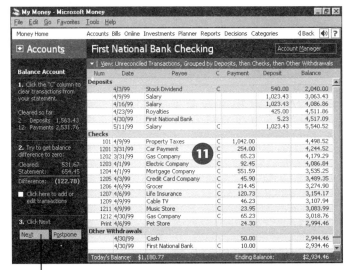

Closing an Account

From time to time you'll want to close an account. If you like, you can make the account inactive, so its records will still be visible and available. You can also delete an account entirely, removing all its records from your computer permanently. Be careful when opting for this last choice: you may have no easy way of restoring the records if you change your mind.

TIP

Change your mind. *Just before Money deletes an account that contains transactions, it asks you if you are certain you want to remove the account. Click the Yes button only if you are positive that you don't want to use the account again.*

Close or Delete an Account

1 Click Accounts on the navigation bar to reveal the Account Manager window.

2 To close an account, right-click the account and choose Account Is Closed from the shortcut menu.

3 To delete an account, select the account and click the Delete Account button. Click Yes when asked to remove the account.

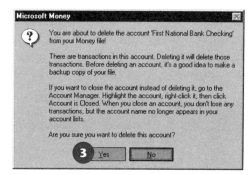

Creating Reports

Reports allow you to summarize and examine spending patterns, your account balances, amounts you owe, investments, and tax information in a form that is easy to understand. You can create on-screen reports to view now, or save them as favorites so you can compare the information on the report with other reports over time.

TIP

Add to favorites. *After you've created a report, you can add it to your favorites list by choosing Add To Favorites from the Favorites menu. Retrieve a report by clicking My Favorites on the Reports & Charts bar, and then choosing the report you want to view.*

Produce a Report

1. Click Reports on the Navigation bar.

2. Click a category on the Reports & Charts bar to view a list of reports and charts.

3. Choose a report from the list.

4. Click the Go To Report/ Chart button to produce the report.

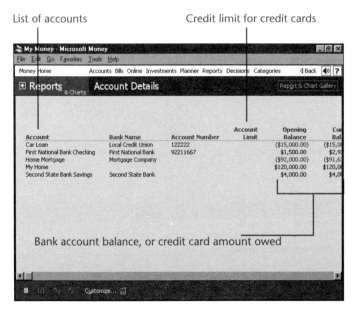

List of accounts

Credit limit for credit cards

Bank account balance, or credit card amount owed

Creating Charts

Charts provide a graphical way of viewing the information gathered by reports. Money lets you create simple bar, line, and pie charts, and customize the fonts, labels, and other elements of the charts. You can view your charts on-screen or print them out for reference.

TIP

Choose fonts. *Careful choice of fonts can make your charts easier to read. Click the Customize button, click the Font tab, and choose the font and size you want.*

Create a Chart

1. Display or create a report you want to make a chart.

2. Click one of the chart buttons at the bottom of the screen.

   ◆ Click the Bar button to create a bar chart.

   ◆ Click the Line button to create a line chart.

   ◆ Click the Pie button to create a pie chart.

3. Click the Customize button and customize the chart.

4. Click the OK button when you are finished.

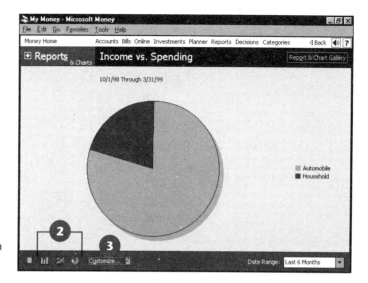

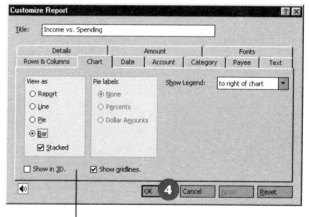

Choose other options to customize the chart.

Printing Reports or Charts

On-screen reports and charts are useful, but you'll often want to print them out for reference, to include in a presentation, or to pass around as a handout.

TIP

Print using patterns. *If you don't have a color printer, you may want to print your charts using black-and-white patterns instead of gray hues. Choose Options from the Tools menu, click the General tab, and then click the Print Charts Using Black & White Patterns check box. Click OK to close the Options dialog box.*

Print a Report or Chart

1 Display the report or chart you want to print.

2 If you like, set up your printer for the report or chart.

◆ Point to Print Setup from the File menu and choose Report and Chart Setup.

◆ Select an Orientation option.

◆ Click the Options button to display the printer's Properties dialog box.

◆ Click OK when you are finished, and then click OK again to finish printer setup.

3 Choose Print from the File menu.

4 Choose the number of copies to print.

5 Click OK to print the report or chart.

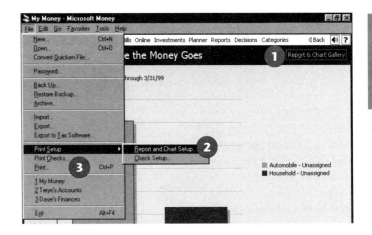

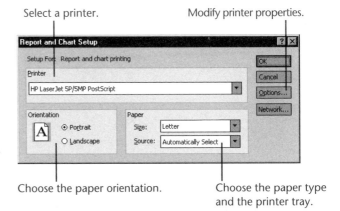

Select a printer.

Modify printer properties.

Choose the paper orientation.

Choose the paper type and the printer tray.

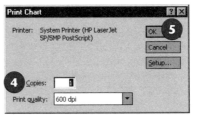

Printing Checks

Although Money saves you plenty of time just by tracking your income and expenses, you can streamline the chore of writing checks by letting Money print them for you. The checks will be neater and less prone to error, because Money uses the information you entered in the register to print the check. To use this feature you must have special preprinted checks and you must understand how to load the checks into your printer.

Print a Check

1. Click Accounts on the navigation bar to reveal the Account Manager.

2. Double-click the account with the check you want to print.

3. Double-click the check you want to print.

4. Choose Print This Transaction from the Number drop-down list.

5. Click the Enter button.

6. If you want to print a name and address on the check, enter it and click OK. Otherwise leave the address screen blank.

7. Repeat steps 3 through 6 for any additional checks you want to print

8. Click Print Checks on the Accounts bar.

9. Enter information about the kind of check forms you will be using, including orientation and the first number on the next check form to be printed.

10. Click Print to print the selected checks.

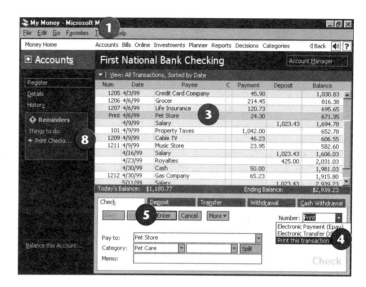

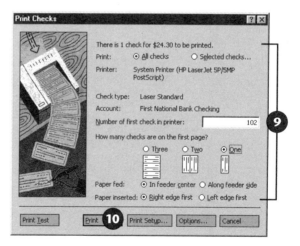

Researching with Encarta Encyclopedia 99

Microsoft Encarta Encyclopedia 99 is your gateway to a wealth of knowledge for business, school, or personal use. It contains more than 35,000 articles with information on everything from the A-Bomb to *Zyzomys argurus* (a species of rat), which you can search or simply browse for pleasure. The text articles are enriched with more than 12,000 media items, including images, sounds, movies, and interactive charts. You'll find a timeline to provide a historical perspective to the people and events of the ages, and maps for exploring our world's geography. Encarta refers to its articles, multimedia clips, and other components as *items*, because it's difficult to find one word to describe all these varied informational elements.

Encarta is a stand-alone application (it must be started separately from Works) that makes learning fun. Interactive collages, a MindMaze game, and other features engage inquisitive minds in activities that are challenging as well as entertaining. Best of all, Encarta always remains current. You can go online to download article updates and Web links that relate to the articles to provide the freshest facts. Additional resources on the Internet can provide in-depth information. This chapter will help you learn Encarta's basic features quickly, so you can begin browsing articles, conducting research, and exploring the multimedia clips.

Viewing Encarta's Screen

Type a word or phrase to search for here.

Move forward or backward among articles and other elements.

Add an article or item to your Favorites list.

Search for articles using the Pinpointer search tool.

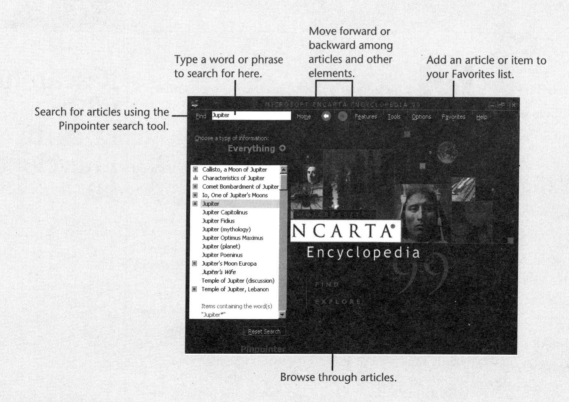

Browse through articles.

Searching for Information

Encarta offers two ways to access its information. You can click Find on Encarta's home screen to search for specific facts or click Explore on the home screen to browse Encarta's articles in a more free-form mode. With more than 500,000 index entries, Encarta is bound to have a relevant cross-reference to help you find the information you need. As you conduct your research, Encarta gives you the choice of searching through all the material it contains or just articles, videos, maps, sound clips, or other categories of information. When you search by keywords, Encarta looks for the words in the titles of the articles and other elements, in the words' index entries, and in the text of the articles themselves.

Begin a Search

1 If the Encarta home page is not displayed, click Home on the menu bar.

2 Click Find on the menu bar to open the Pinpointer, Encarta's search tool.

3 Type an entire word or phrase or the first few characters of it, or pose your query in the form of a question (such as *What is the capital of Ghana?*).

4 Scroll through the list to find the item you want.

5 If you want to search only for certain kinds of material, click the arrow button and choose the kind of content you want, such as animations, articles, or charts.

6 When you find the item you want to view, double-click it.

7 If you're viewing a longer article, click a section number to jump directly to that section of the article.

8 When you've finished viewing the material, click Home on the menu bar to return to the Encarta home screen.

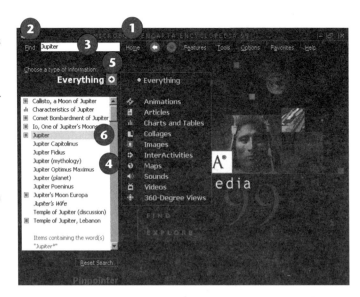

14

Searching by Location or Time Frame

If you prefer to locate information based on its geographic location or its time in history, Encarta can sort information by location or date. You'll find these features useful when researching a particular place or era.

TIP

Read article about an event. *While browsing the Timeline, click an icon marking an event to view a short article about that event.*

Search by Time

1. Choose Timeline from the Features menu.

2. Click Find An Event.

   ◆ Click the Event button to view a list of events in alphabetical order.

   ◆ Click the Date button to view a list of events in chronological order.

3. Click an event to display its location on the timeline.

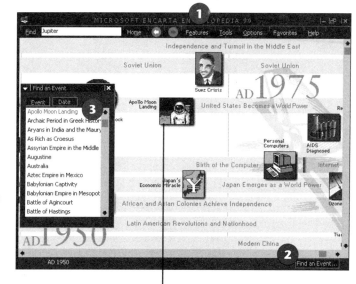

Timeline displays the selected event.

Move around a map. *Once you've zoomed in to the area you want, you can scroll around the map by placing the mouse pointer at any side or corner of the map.*

Read an article about a place. *Click a place's name. If an article is available about that place, Go To Article appears in white on the shortcut menu. Click Go To Article to jump directly to more information about the place.*

Search by Place

1. If necessary, click the Home button on the menu bar to return to Encarta's opening screen.

2. To search by place name, click Find on the menu bar and type the name of a place.

3. To locate using a map, choose World Maps from the Features menu, and repeatedly click the map until the place you want is displayed. Each time you click, the view of the map is magnified.

14

Browsing Articles

You don't have to use the Pinpointer search tool to look for information. You can browse general topics, such as Science or History, and select subtopics in them until you reach a selection of articles that interests you. Encarta's Explore tool is an excellent alternative to the Pinpointer when you don't know exactly what you want, or you simply want to scan the material for pleasure.

> **TIP**
>
> **Returns to more general topic.** *As you delve into Encarta's topics, subtopics are arrayed along the outside edges of the screen, while the previous general topic level moves to the center. Click the center topic at any time to return to the previous level.*

> **TIP**
>
> **Restart your exploration.** *Click Explore on the home screen to begin a new exploration from the top level.*

Explore Articles

1. Click Home on the menu bar, and then click the Explore link in the lower-middle section of the home page.

2. Click Science, History, Geography, Social Science, or Humanities to choose a topic to explore.

3. Keep clicking subtopics until Encarta stops offering additional subtopics.

4. Hover the mouse pointer over each item to produce a description of that item.

5. Double-click any item to display it.

6. View any clips, pictures, article sections or cross-references.

7. To move back to any topic level, click the Back or Forward buttons until you reach the level you want.

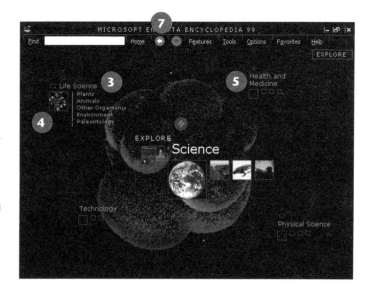

Cacti in the Sonoran Desert
Many varieties of cacti grow in Arizona's Sonoran Desert. Shown here are the organ pipe and saguaro varieties.
David Orbock/Village Gallery

Exploring Cross-References

If a single article or other item doesn't provide all the information you need, you can explore related articles in the encyclopedia by following cross-references. Encarta provides three kinds of references: to articles, to other items, and to Web-based information resources. Each article usually has links to other articles with more detail about specific aspects of the topic. Encarta also lists animations, sound clips, maps, and other material relevant to your topic. It also points to Internet information sources, including Encarta's Online Library, Encarta's Online Web links, and searches of other destinations on the World Wide Web.

Find Related Information

1. Click Home on the menu bar, if necessary, to display Encarta's home screen, and then click Find on the menu bar to open Encarta's Pinpointer search tool.

2. Type a word or phrase or the first few characters to display a list of articles on your topic.

3. Double-click an article to display it.

4. In the right column, view the lists of related articles and multimedia.

    ◆ If you're connected to the Internet, you can also click one of the Web resources that appear.

5. Click a cross-reference to jump to that item.

6. Continue following cross-references until you've viewed all the information you want.

7. Click the Back or Forward button at any time to return to another page.

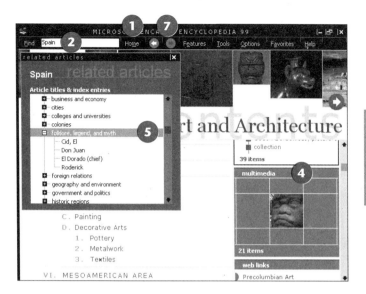

Taking Notes

As you collect information from articles, you'll often want to print the facts you find or copy them to another document to save as notes. Encarta makes it easy to print or copy any article or only selected text. If you copy text, you can paste it in a document you've created with Word 97 or the Works word processor tool.

TIP

Copy only an image. *To copy just an illustration, right-click the image and choose Copy from the shortcut menu.*

Take Notes

1. If you want to copy some or all text from an article, open a blank document in Word 97 or the Works word processor tool.

2. Use the Pinpointer search tool or browse to the article you want to print or copy.

3. If you want to copy or print part of an article or a single image, select that text or image by dragging with the mouse.

4. Choose Print or Copy from the Options menu.

5. If you're copying text, click either the Whole Article Text or the Selected Text button. If you're copying an image, choose either Whole Caption Text or Image.

6. Click the Copy or Print button.

7. If you've copied an article or image, switch to the word processing document.

8. Choose Paste from the Edit menu.

9. Return to Encarta and search for additional articles to take notes from.

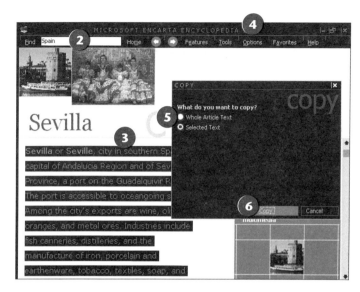

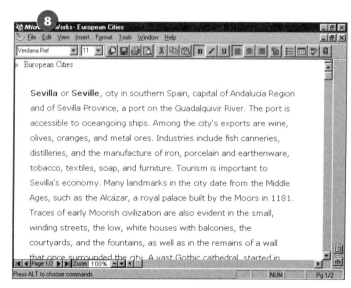

Adding Items to Your Favorites List

Encarta's Favorites list is an excellent tool for organizing your research. You can create folders for the topics you are studying and add relevant pages to those folders as you explore Encarta's information. For example, for a report on the Civil War, you might create a folder called Civil War, and subfolders within it named Lincoln, Grant, Lee, and Gettysburg. Any article or other item can be added to your Favorites list with a few clicks.

> **TIP**
>
> **View Favorites.** *To retrieve an iteme from your Favorites folder, click Favorites on the menu bar and choose a favorite article, image, or folder.*

Save a Favorite

1. Find the article or other item you want to store in a Favorites folder.

2. Choose Add To Favorites from the Favorites menu.

    ◆ To place the item in a new folder, click the New Folder button and type a name for the folder.

3. If you want, type your own title for the article or image.

4. Select a location in the Create In box.

5. Click OK to save the Favorite and return to the article.

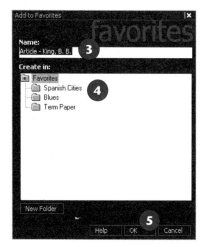

Organizing Your Favorites

The ability to organize your Favorites by moving them among folders is a valuable research tool. For example, you can keep articles for a research project in a General folder until you've had a chance to read them and decide which Favorites folder best suits your project. You can freely create new folders, delete unwanted folders, and move articles and media back and forth among them as your research continues.

TIP

Find a Favorite. *If your collection of Favorites is large, Encarta can search through the folders to find the one you want. Choose Organize Favorites from the Favorites menu. Right-click the folder you want to search and choose Find. Type a word or part of a word from the title of the Favorite you're looking for and click Find Now. Choose the Favorite you want from the list.*

Organize Favorites

1 Click Organize Favorites on the Favorites menu.

2 Click the New Folder button if you want to create a new folder.

3 Double-click folders to find articles in them.

4 Drag favorite items from one folder to another to reorganize them.

5 Click the Close button when you've finished reorganizing your Favorites.

Enjoying Multimedia

One significant advantage Encarta has over printed encyclopedias is its ability to integrate informative video clips, animations, sound clips, and interactive segments with its articles. You can read an article about a topic, such as bird identification, and then view video clips of birds, hear their songs, and step through an interactive exercise to help put what you've learned into practice.

TIP

Locate clips quickly. *To search only for video or audio clips, choose Sounds or Videos from the Pinpointer's Choose A Type Of Information menu.*

SEE ALSO

For information on learning with interactive exercises, see "Learning Interactively" on page 246.

View Multimedia Clips

1. Locate a video or audio clip you want to play.

2. Double-click the clip.

3. Use the player's controls to start, pause, move forward quickly, or rewind the video or audio clip.

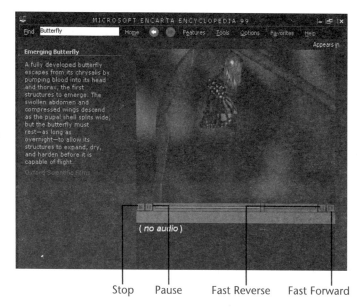

Stop   Pause   Fast Reverse   Fast Forward

14

Learning Interactively

Encarta's compact computer learning elements, called *InterActivities*, are a great way to involve yourself actively in the learning process. These modules use sight, sound, demonstrations, and other tools to present information interactively. You can play a game, assemble a dinosaur's skeleton, or build a population chart for your state.

Use an Interactive Exercise

1. Choose InterActivities from the Features menu.

2. Pass the mouse pointer over an InterActivity on the list for a preview.

3. Click the name of the InterActivity to begin.

4. Read the instructions and complete the activity.

5. Click the Back or Home button when you are finished with the InterActivity.

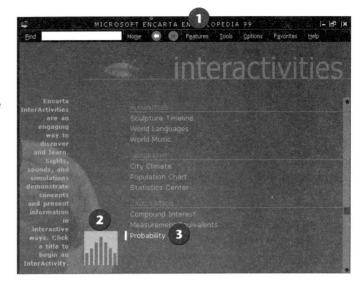

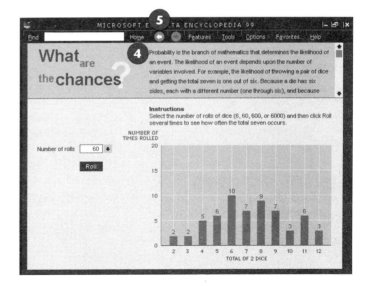

Index

The manuscript for this book was prepared and submitted to Microsoft Press in electronic form. Text files were prepared using Microsoft Word 97. Pages were composed by Susan Glinert using PageMaker for Windows, with text in Stone Sans and display type in Stone Serif and Stone Serif Semibold. Composed pages were delivered to the printer as electronic prepress files.

Cover Designer
Tim Girvin Design

Compositor and
Graphic Layout Artist
Susan Glinert

Copy Editor
J.W. Olsen

Indexer
Scott Nolan Hollerith

Powerful
Web design tools
made easy.

U.S.A. **$24.99**
U.K.   £22.99
Canada $35.99
ISBN 1-57231-836-8

WEB ADVERTISING AND MARKETING BY DESIGN provides hands-on, step-by-step instruction to help create dynamic advertising and promotional projects for the World Wide Web—whether or not you're an advertising or marketing professional. The book presents more than a dozen sample projects that you can customize and use, tapping powerful features from the latest Microsoft® Web design and content creation tools, including FrontPage®, Image Composer, GIF Animator, Microsoft Internet Explorer, and Microsoft Word. Each chapter discusses a project's theme and goals along with its size and scope, and then highlights key steps to help get your project organized and under way. Every project presents carefully constructed examples and precise information on creating effective graphic and text-based content.

Microsoft Press

Microsoft Press offers *comprehensive* learning solutions to help **new users,** **power users, and professionals** get the most from *Microsoft technology.*

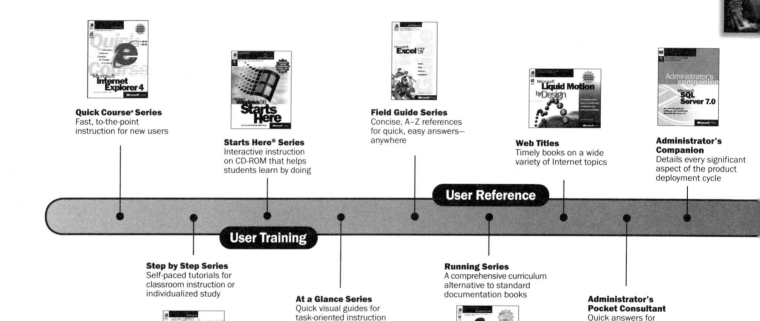

Quick Course® Series
Fast, to-the-point
instruction for new users

Starts Here® Series
Interactive instruction
on CD-ROM that helps
students learn by doing

Field Guide Series
Concise, A–Z references
for quick, easy answers—
anywhere

Web Titles
Timely books on a wide
variety of Internet topics

Administrator's Companion
Details every significant
aspect of the product
deployment cycle

User Reference

User Training

Step by Step Series
Self-paced tutorials for
classroom instruction or
individualized study

At a Glance Series
Quick visual guides for
task-oriented instruction

Running Series
A comprehensive curriculum
alternative to standard
documentation books

Administrator's Pocket Consultant
Quick answers for
everyday network
management issues

Microsoft Press® products are available worldwide wherever quality computer books are sold. For more information, contact your book or computer retailer, software reseller, or local Microsoft Sales Office, or visit our Web site at mspress.microsoft.com. To locate your nearest source for Microsoft Press products, or to order directly, call 1-800-MSPRESS in the U.S. (in Canada, call 1-800-268-2222).

Prices and availability dates are subject to change.

With **over 200** *print, multimedia, and online*

resources—whatever your training or reference need or

learning style, **we've got a solution**

to help you *start faster and go farther.*

Notes from the Field
Microsoft Consulting Services'
best practices for supporting
enterprise technology

Readiness Reviews
Microsoft Certified
Professional exam
practice on CD-ROM

**Microsoft®
Professional Editions**
Technical information
straight from the source

**Microsoft
Programming Series**
The foundations of
software development

Professional

Developers

**Technical
References**
Highly focused
IT reference
and solutions

**Strategic
Technology Series**
Easy-to-read overviews
for decision makers

**Microsoft Certified
Professional Training Kits**
The Microsoft Official
Curriculum for certification
exams

Resource Kits
Comprehensive technical
information and tools to
plan, deploy, and manage
Microsoft technology

Developer Learning Tools
Learning packages designed to
build mastery of programming
fundamentals

Look for them at your bookstore or computer store today!

Microsoft® *Press*

mspress.microsoft.com

mspress.microsoft.com

Microsoft Press Online is your road map to the best available print and multimedia materials—resources that will help you maximize the effectiveness of Microsoft® software products. Our goal is making it easy and convenient for you to find exactly the Microsoft Press® book or interactive product you need, as well as bringing you the latest in training and certification materials from Microsoft Press.

Where do you want to go today?®